GHOSTS OF AUSTIN, TEXAS

WHO THEY ARE
AND WHERE TO FIND THEM

Fiona Broome

4880 Lower Valley Road   Atglen, Pennsylvania   19310

DEDICATION

This book is dedicated to the many spirits of Austin, Texas, and the stories that they wanted me to tell in this book. May they find the peace and contentment that they seek, and—if they wish it—enjoy happier interactions with the living.

Published by Schiffer Publishing Ltd.
4880 Lower Valley Road
Atglen, PA 19310
Phone: (610) 593-1777; Fax: (610) 593-2002
E-mail: Info@schifferbooks.com

For the largest selection of fine reference books on this and related subjects, please visit our web site at
www.schifferbooks.com
We are always looking for people to write books on new and related subjects. If you have an idea for a book please contact us at the above address.

This book may be purchased from the publisher.
Include $3.95 for shipping.
Please try your bookstore first.
You may write for a free catalog.

In Europe, Schiffer books are distributed by
Bushwood Books
6 Marksbury Ave.
Kew Gardens
Surrey TW9 4JF England
Phone: 44 (0) 20 8392-8585; Fax: 44 (0) 20 8392-9876
E-mail: info@bushwoodbooks.co.uk
Website: www.bushwoodbooks.co.uk
Free postage in the U.K., Europe; air mail at cost.

Designed by Mark David Bowyer
Type set in Cancun / New Baskerville BT

ISBN: 978-0-7643-2680-6
Printed in China

CONTENTS

INTRODUCTION

Downtown Austin, Texas may have more ghosts per block than any city in America. Visitors can encounter dozens of ghosts of the Wild West within blocks of most central Austin hotels.

If you have only twenty-four hours in Austin, here's how to get the most from your ghost hunting:

• Start by visiting some of Austin's cemeteries early in the morning while the mist is still lifting. Choose either the historical graves at Oakwood and Oakwood Annex cemeteries, or the thousands of unmarked graves in a field representing the Austin State Hospital Cemetery. If the gates are locked, you can easily take great, eerie photos through the fence. See Chapter Three for directions and more information about the most haunted graves.

• Then, check into the opulent—and haunted—Driskill Hotel. Explore its many haunted rooms, corridors, and floors. Pay special attention to the fifth floor and the lobby; both have an abundance of ghost stories that you can read about in Chapter One.

•   Go across the street to the Austin Visitor Information Center. Pick up their free Historic Walking Tours booklets, and ask about the latest ghost sightings around the city.

•   Before lunch, tour the Capitol and the Governor's Mansion. Both sites report numerous apparitions and strange sounds, even at midday. (See Chapter One for details.)

•   Visit the Spaghetti Warehouse at 117 West Fourth Street for lunch. Ask your waiter about their ghosts… There may be dozens of them—including noisy ghosts and apparitions—from the basement to the upstairs. In the nineteenth century, this was the home of a popular brothel.

•   After lunch, stroll up the street for happy hour at Oilcan Harry's upscale gay bar, frequented by the ghost of madam Blanche Dumont. Or, visit Fado Irish Pub across the street, where spirits from an old theater socialize with ghosts of shameless nineteenth century hussies. Learn more about the independent women of early Austin—and their ghosts—in "Austin's Entertainment District: From Red Lights to Red Carpet."

•   In mid-afternoon, plan your own cemetery tour using the list in Chapter Three. The Austin area has hundreds of small cemeteries; watch for them in unlikely places by the side of the road or tucked behind strip malls.

• Late in the day, visit Whole Foods famous headquarters store for great take-out food, or shop at the haunted Central Market on Lamar Boulevard, near Shoal Creek. Take your picnic into beautiful (but ghostly) Shoal Creek and read about the Shoal Creek Curse in Chapter One. If you linger in the park until dusk, you may see or smell the phantom campfires of Civil War ghosts.

• Around dusk, head towards the Congress Avenue Bridge and find a viewing spot on either side of the river. Every night between mid-March and early November, over a million bats fly from under the bridge in search of food. It's a magnificent but creepy sight. Read more about the bats, and other places to see them, in Chapter Four.

• After the bat display, head back to your favorite cemeteries for after-dark photos. Remember that most Texas cemeteries close at night, but you can take photos through the fences for great orb and vortex pictures. (Learn more about taking ghost photos in the appendix at the back of this book.)

• Finally, return to the Driskill Hotel and get ready for a boisterous night on the town. With popular, haunted bars such as Buffalo Billiards and B. D. Riley's, you'll find friendly faces—some of them ghosts—throughout Austin's famous entertainment and warehouse districts. You may also enjoy one of Austin's ghost tours, to learn about the darker side of the city… and the ghosts that linger there.

• Before climbing into bed for a good night's sleep, stroll to Fifth Street in case you catch a glimpse of Susannah Wilkerson Dickinson's ghost at her old home near the Hilton Hotel. Her little house is next to O. Henry's home, which may also be haunted.

• Or, if you're a night owl with nerves of steel, visit the grisly, haunted locations where Jack the Ripper took the lives of at least seven people, and perhaps as many as twenty. For more about this little-known side of Austin's history, see Chapter Two.

If you have an extra day or two in Austin, you'll find dozens of other haunted locations described in this book. From the ghosts of the UT Tower tragedy to the legendary spirits of the Alamo, Austin and vicinity can provide the scariest days and nights of your life.

—Fiona Broome

CHAPTER ONE:
HAUNTED AUSTIN LANDMARKS

THE DRISKILL HOTEL

There are two different kinds of haunted hotels.

First, there are hotels so haunted, you'll be lucky to get any sleep while you're there.

Then, there are wonderful places such as the Driskill Hotel, which is charmingly haunted and still assures you of a full and refreshing night's sleep.

Their ghosts are easy to find if you go looking for them, but they'll leave you alone if you prefer to rest.

The Driskill Hotel's early history was turbulent. Just six months after it opened its doors in 1886, it closed… and then reopened five months later.

Six years later, the Driskill was back on the auction block, and bought by a group of British investors. Less than a year after that, the Brits closed shop and the hotel was sold again.

This pattern continued for many years. The hotel opened, then it closed, then it opened again, and so on. Most recently, in 1999, new owners restored the hotel to its original splendor. The Driskill's turn-of-the-century décor is now elegant beyond description. It's no surprise that the Driskill Hotel appears on almost every "top ten" list of America's best and grandest hotels.

It's also one of America's most haunted hotels, and a favorite place to stay if you want to be treated like royalty but also enjoy a few "good scares" during your visit. At least a dozen ghosts haunt the Driskill.

Ghost orbs at Austin's haunted Driskill Hotel. *Photo by the author.*

Peter J. Lawless may be the Driskill Hotel's most persistent ghost. During his lifetime, he was certainly one of its most enthusiastic guests. He lived in the hotel from its opening in 1886 until his death, no matter who owned the hotel and whether it was open or not. Even when the hotel was closed, he didn't leave. He had his own key to the building, and used candles for light when the power was turned off.

Researcher Pete Haviland of Lone Star Spirits Paranormal Investigations has investigated the Driskill Hotel and comments, "Be careful getting off the elevator—you may run into Mr. Lawless checking his watch."

He's right. Mr. Lawless is most often encountered around the elevators. Some people see him as clearly as if he's still alive. His brown suit looks only a little out-of-date. However, many hotel guests feel that he's looking right through them... as if they're the ghosts, and not him.

More often, people sense Mr. Lawless rather than see him. When they step out of the elevator, they feel a sudden breeze as if someone had just walked past.

The elevators also stop at random floors for no apparent reason. In the elevators, guests unexpectedly visit the top floor, but when the doors open, no one is there. Mr. Lawless may be responsible, or it could be a prank by Colonel Driskill, also known as Jesse Lincoln Driskill, the man who founded the hotel. His portrait is in the hotel lobby.

Colonel Driskill is a very popular ghost. He's responsible for the cigar aroma on the upper floors. Colonel Driskill enjoys turning lights on and off in some guest rooms, just for fun. Try not to let this annoy you, or he'll just keep playing these pranks.

The Driskill Hotel's upper floors are probably the most haunted. Guests hear the sound of people dancing or children playing overhead, even when no one is there. It's never loud enough that guests complain, but when they comment about the noise, the staff often smiles, knowing that the ghosts are having a party again.

Then there's the "Wild West" apparition of a cowboy. He fades in and out like a grinning Cheshire cat, startling guests. He can turn up anywhere in the hotel, including guest rooms and dining areas. No one knows his identity, but he's one of the ghosts that inspired the Concrete Blonde song, "Ghost of a Texas Ladies Man."

Back downstairs, the old vault in the hotel lobby is haunted with unique ghosts: They're visiting to put money into the vault.

Within days of his inauguration in March 1933, President Franklin Roosevelt abruptly closed all American banks for about a month to halt the panic over failed investments.

Guests at the Driskill Hotel were stranded without cash, but the Driskill's manager, W. L. Stark, came to their rescue. He opened the hotel safe and started handing out money to those who needed it. He didn't ask anyone to sign a promissory note. He simply asked them to return the money when the crisis was over. And, all of them did, sometimes adding a little extra to say thank you.

If you visit the small room where the vault is today, you'll feel a sense of great wealth, as if people are walking to and fro in their silks and top hats. Some speculate that they're still visiting the Driskill to add a little more cash and to repay the hotel's generosity.

After you leave the vault, be sure to watch the marble staircase almost opposite it. The ghost of a little girl descends the stairs from the upper right side, and laughs as she follows a ball bouncing merrily in front of her.

According to legend, she fell down those stairs to her death, while her father—a politician—was in a meeting.

A ghostly little girl plays on these stairs in the lobby of the Driskill Hotel. Near the top of the stairs, the orb captured in this photo may represent her spirit. *Photo by the author.*

She's not the only little girl haunting the hotel. Ask the staff about the haunted painting of a little girl in an old fashioned, high-waisted dress. In this painting, the child holds flowers in her left hand and a letter tied with a ribbon in her right. Very strange energy emanates from it.

The eyes of the girl seem to follow you, no matter where you are. If you stand in front of the painting and look straight into her eyes, you may feel slightly disoriented. Some people describe their heels lifting slightly. Others simply get the chills when they're near this painting.

When I visited the Driskill Hotel, the painting was displayed in a fifth floor corridor, not far from the Bridal Suite. It was probably intended as a charming and innocent painting, but in the hotel, it seems almost sinister.

The ghost of a former hotel housekeeper—perhaps from the very early twentieth century—still works at the Driskill. Sometimes she's an apparition in a long, old-fashioned dress with a slim skirt.

More often, guests notice only what she's doing: She likes to rearrange the flowers in the many displays around the hotel, especially at the lobby and on the mezzanine. If the flowers seem to move by themselves, you've seen the ghostly housekeeper at work.

Most of the Driskill Hotel's ghosts are playful, and they pulled a large-scale prank when I first toured the hotel.

Since I'm a medium, I often "see" haunted locations as if looking through the eyes of the ghosts. A translucent, historical image seems displayed between me and the modern-day surroundings. History seems physically closer, but not quite as real.

In the quiet elegance of the hotel's Citadel Club, I noticed modern light bulbs in the wall fixtures. As a medium, I could "see" candles in similar fixtures, all around the room.

As if on cue, the lights flickered. I assumed that they were designed to do that, to mimic turn-of-the-century candles. Aloud, I commented, "Those lights should be flickering."

Then, the power went out altogether, and I heard a deep, eerie chuckle from behind mc. I turned to look, thinking that it was a hotel worker, but no one was there.

My tour guide explained that other parts of the hotel were being renovated, and perhaps the workmen had turned off the power in the room to work on wiring.

A few minutes later, we learned that "something odd" had happened to the power main, and the entire hotel would be without power for at least 16 hours, and perhaps as long as three days.

As a ghost hunter, I know that the spirits can affect electrical equipment. In fact, that's a common sign of a ghost: TVs turn themselves on and off, lights flicker and go out, and so on. So, I was surprised when the Driskill's spirits took this opportunity to make their influence known, but I was not as rattled as the other guests.

My guide and I continued to tour the hotel, relying on the hotel's emergency lights.

Our next stop was the ladies room near the hotel's well-equipped fitness center. Apparently, the small bathroom is haunted. One guest reported that when she tried to leave the toilet stall, the door pulled against her for a few minutes. Finally, something released the handle and she was able to leave. That's a typical ghostly prank.

In the darkness—and without normal electrical interference—I measured elevated EMF levels in two areas of the small bathroom. Something definitely haunts there.

After that, my guide and I explored other eerie areas around the hotel.

In the Crystal Room, look for a ghost to ride his horse through the walls. The hotel stables used to be located where a dining room is today.

Upstairs, a spectral security guard patrols the halls. According to some, he was murdered while working for the hotel, but still shows up for his shift each day.

I've observed him around the fifth floor. He's slightly see-through and you'll notice him ahead of you, just turning the corner to vanish from sight. He walks briskly, as if he's hiding from guests. Or, perhaps he's on his way to check something important.

On a lower floor, a private and spacious suite of hotel rooms recently reopened after being sealed for over fifty years. No one would tell me why the rooms were sealed, though there were rumors of a suicide or murder in the very early twentieth century.

The suite was only slightly haunted when I visited during remodeling, but there's something dark and gurgling as you walk along the hallway towards it. I know that "gurgling" is an odd word for it, but... Well, you can experience it yourself if you stay at the Driskill.

Near that suite, some people have seen the late President Lyndon Baines Johnson. He watched election results at the Driskill Hotel, and often celebrated there as well. He's described as a translucent figure of a lanky man relaxing against one wall, or sitting in a chair where the light seems unusually low. His distinctive smile and friendliness make his identity obvious.

My favorite haunted room in the Driskill Hotel is also near the reopened suite and where LBJ has been sighted.

The Maximilian Room is a luxurious reception room with comfortable sofas and the hotel's original, sparkling chandeliers.

This room's enormous "Carlotta" mirrors will intrigue most ghost hunters. They were intended as a gift from Austrian archduke Ferdinand Maximilian to his wife, Carlotta.

After years of civil war in Mexico, conservatives— supported by French military forces—attempted to replace Mexico's elected president Benito Juarez with an emperor, Maximilian. Unfortunately, Maximilian tried to please everyone by proposing a limited monarchy. No one was amused.

Carlotta quickly fled to Europe, begging both Napoleon III and the Pope for help with Mexico. Neither of them wanted further involvement in the civil war.

Carlotta never saw her husband again. In 1867, he was shot and Juarez reclaimed the presidency. However, the emperor left a gift and perhaps a lingering connection to the other side.

Before he died, Maximilian had ordered eight magnificent mirrors from Europe. They sparkle more than most because their reflective surfaces were created with diamond dust. At the top of each enormous mirror, you can see the etched image of Carlotta.

The mirrors never arrived in Mexico, and Carlotta never saw them. She spent the rest of her life in seclusion in Italy, under the care of physicians. Meanwhile, when news of Maximilian's death reach the carrier, the mirrors were left in San Antonio. There was no point in delivering them.

The Driskill Hotel acquired these opulent and eerie mirrors in the 1930s. Today, they line the walls of the Maximilian Room.

Ghost hunters know that mirrors can act as portals to the other side. Ghosts are frequently seen in reflections. However, the history and placement of these mirrors make them especially eerie. The mirrors reflect each other, amplifying their supernatural powers so that they can display apparitions and haunted images.

Although the mirrors are otherwise identical, pay special attention as you enter the Maximilian Room. On the long wall at a right angle to the door, study the mirror nearest to you. You'll soon sense that it has more otherworldly energy than the others. I don't know why it's so different, but it's a very powerful sensation.

Sit on the sofa and observe it out of the corner of your eye as you look around the room. Many visitors see images flickering across the glass. It's as if people are crossing the room and are reflected in the mirror…when no one else is in the room.

The Driskill Hotel is easily one of America's most haunted hotels. It's also one of the world's most opulent hotels, and well worth visiting whether or not you're eager for a "good scare."

If you look for ghosts at the Driskill Hotel, you'll probably find them.

AUSTIN'S HAUNTED ENTERTAINMENT DISTRICT—FROM RED LIGHTS TO RED CARPET

If you're looking for an area where almost every building has a ghost story, you'll find it in downtown Austin's entertainment and warehouse districts.

This neighborhood once featured a brash display of saloons, brothels, and gambling halls. Though the fringe neighborhoods may have been tawdry, downtown Austin was opulent thanks to successful saloons, gambling halls, and brothels. For much of Austin's early history, these businesses were tolerated and sometimes encouraged for the income that they brought to the city.

Through the early twentieth century, prostitution flourished in Austin, especially in the area called Guy Town.

Guy Town was the nickname for Austin's red light district, also called Ward 1 or "Mexico." It was the most colorful part of town, and—with over a hundred Austin prostitutes selling their wares in 1880—the neighborhood was very popular.

In its early days, Guy Town's borders were formed by the river, Guadalupe Street, Colorado Street, and Fifth Street. That's where most of Austin's ghosts are. However, many nearby streets—especially Sixth Street (formerly the sometimes-infamous Pecan Street)—are also profoundly haunted.

Prostitution was a popular and lucrative occupation for independent-minded Texas women. Any young woman could launch a career since Texas' legal age of consent was just ten years old. By age eighteen, a woman could earn enough to start her own brothel or dance hall.

Austin's City Council tried to ban prostitution in 1870, outlawing "fandangoes" or dance houses "where lewd women or persons who have no visible means of support are admitted."

However, until a few anti-prostitution zealots shut down Guy Town around 1913, the men and women of Austin accepted the reality, necessity, and benefits of their red-light district.

Between 1876 and 1879, only nine people were charged with "running a house of ill-repute." In the 1900 U. S. Census, many women openly listed their occupations as "prostitute."

British-born Blanche Dumont was one of the most famous Austin madams at the turn of the century. She's probably the best known ghost at Oilcan Harry's bar on Fourth Street.

Blanche Dumont had a colorful history, starting in her native England.

In the 1900 census, Ms. Dumont described herself as the owner of a boarding house at 211 West Fourth Street. Her guests included a chambermaid, a porter, and four prostitutes. Three of Ms. Dumont's girls had probably accompanied her from New York.

Blanche's ghost is seen on the dance floor at Oilcan Harry's, as well as many other corners of this upscale gay men's bar.

Notes from the other side

Blanche Dumont wants to speak her mind. She feels that she was Austin's pre-eminent "boarding house madam," as she calls herself, and she wants to be heard.

Looking back, she is still upset that she never really found romance. She felt that she provided so much comfort to so many men, she was owed a karmic debt of gratitude in the form of true love. At the time of her death—which was sudden—she was about to do something extraordinary for a woman. She's not clear about what that was, as if she's still holding her cards very close. But, she's now in a state of uncertainty about her life's accomplishments. In part, it's because she's not sure that she's still attractive. Her brothel became Oilcan Harry's, a gay bar where most of the men don't seem attracted to her, even when she manifests as a very real-looking blonde in ivory silk underwear.

However, Ms. Dumont is not the only famous madam haunting modern-day Austin.

Della Robinson was another very popular brothel owner, and mixed comfortably with members of the upper class. Wealthy Eula Phillips, a descendant of Texas' elite "Old Three Hundred," amused herself by working as a prostitute in Ms. Robinson's house.

However, Belle Brown was less happy with her employment there. She used morphine to commit suicide in her room at the brothel. She and Ms. Robinson are among the many ghosts seen after dark on the streets around Austin's entertainment district.

If you're looking for ghosts from the old red-light district, be sure to visit Austin's City Hall complex at 301 West Second Street. This innovative limestone and copper clad building was unveiled late in 2004, and it occupies four blocks that once included some of early Austin's wildest casinos and houses of prostitution.

It seems that the ghosts don't like the sanitized, respectable city structure covering their old stomping ground. A variety of apparitions—men and women—have been seen around those blocks, according to reports beginning in the 1960s.

One of the City Hall's most popular ghosts is called Adelle. In the late nineteenth century, she was an outspoken prostitute who worked in several brothels, and aspired to own her own saloon with a dining area, casino and bar downstairs, and elegant rooms for the girls upstairs.

She was also a suffragette and campaigned for women's right to vote. Unfortunately, her fiancé didn't agree with her liberated views. He shot her in her bed one afternoon, immediately after a customer had left her room.

Adelle walks the sidewalks at City Hall, and sometimes her outline can be seen in the third-floor window. Most people see her as a pinkish or golden blur in their peripheral vision, or they hear the rustle of her silk gown as she walks.

One Halloween night in the late 1970s, a couple saw Adelle during her nightly stroll around City Hall Plaza.

Adelle approached the man and asked him to light her hand-rolled cigarette. When the gentleman declined, explaining that he didn't smoke, Adelle glared at him. She tossed her head indignantly as she glanced at his companion, and then she vanished. Until Adelle disappeared, the couple didn't realize that she was a ghost.

However, you don't need to travel that far to see Austin's ghosts. Almost every club and restaurant in downtown Austin seems to have a ghostly history.

Buffalo Billiards, at 201 East Sixth Street, is less than a block from the haunted Driskill Hotel. In 1861, Buffalo Billiards' site opened as the Missouri Hotel, Austin's first "boarding house."

Right:
Buffalo Billiard's was once the site of a brothel. It's still haunted by the ghosts of nineteenth century prostitutes who enjoy the boisterous atmosphere at this popular bar. *Photo by the author.*

Today, the 22,000 square foot building is still frequented by the spirits of the wild and colorful women who worked there. On the ground floor, you may see one of them in a low-cut pink satin gown edged with black lace. Upstairs, the ghosts appear more brazenly, wearing little more than a shawl and gartered stockings. Look for the flash of shiny silk underwear out of the corner of your eye.

The ghosts of the brothel's patrons are among the rowdiest in Austin. They reportedly leave pool sticks and billiard balls strewn around the popular club, even after the building has been cleaned and locked for the night.

Across the street from Buffalo Billiards, you may see a few ghostly guests seated near the bar in B. D. Riley's at 204 East Sixth Street. One popular spirit will lean towards you and, in a whiskey-soaked stage whisper, announce that he'd like to buy you—or perhaps the entire bar—a drink. Then, he starts to stand up to make this announcement, and vanishes. Some patrons see him at the door, waiting for a moment and then fading as if he was never there.

Right:
This historical plaque marks the haunted Hannig Building. *Photo by the author.*

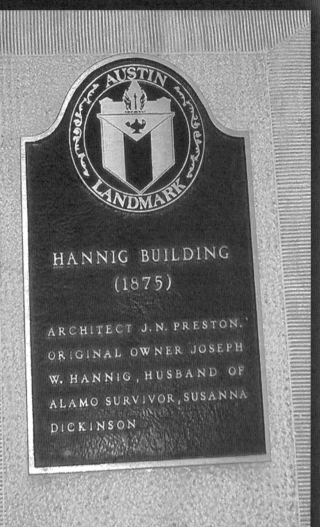

AUSTIN LANDMARK

HANNIG BUILDING
(1875)

ARCHITECT J. N. PRESTON.
ORIGINAL OWNER JOSEPH
W. HANNIG, HUSBAND OF
ALAMO SURVIVOR, SUSANNA
DICKINSON

On that same block at 206 East Sixth Street, look up at the top floor of the Hannig Building. Joseph W. Hannig was the widower of Alamo survivor Susannah Wilkerson Dickinson. After dark, he's seen gazing out the window of the building that bears his name. He's about two feet away from the window and looking down on the street below. Some claim that he disapproves of what's going on below. Others say that he's cautiously watching for Susannah, whose ghost is more often seen around her former residence at Brush Square near the Hilton Hotel.

Joseph Hannig haunts the top floor of the building that bears his name. In this photo, a ghostly orb hovers over the window where he is often seen. *Photo by the author.*

Logan's trendy sports bar at 200 East Sixth Street may have a ghost on its second floor, as well. Like the Hannig Building, a male ghost frequents this site. He's known for moving glasses, swinging doors, and he's infamous for his unearthly laughter.

Just a few doors away, the Old Pecan Street Café at 310 East Sixth Street is haunted by another ghostly figure. She usually appears in Victorian clothing, gazes at you, and quickly vanishes.

If you went from door to door in Austin's entertainment and warehouse districts, you'd probably find ghost stories at more than half of the shops, clubs, and restaurants.

Austin's famous "Lady in Blue" haunts a former brothel site at 407 East Seventh Street. She doesn't seem to react to the modern day world around her, but vanishes if anyone gets too near to her. At that same location, others have heard ghostly music, and felt startling, cool breezes. These reports come from visitors and people who work there, as well as investigators from Lone Star Spirits.

At 412D Congress Avenue, the Speakeasy lives up to its historical name. At this self-proclaimed "swanky joint," ghosts of the past appear in the club's elevator. The spirits also slam doors, shout loudly, and run up and down the stairs to their Rooftop Terrace.

Along Guadalupe Street, especially near the Clay Pit Grill & Curry House at the 1600 block, people hear ghostly parties in empty rooms, and encounter business owners and patrons from the nineteenth century.

The Spaghetti Warehouse at 117 West Fourth Street is one of Austin's most reliably haunted restaurants. Look for the figure of a man—or sometimes just his legs—around the vault. An employee encountered the ghost of an elderly woman in the basement. She jumped at him, and then vanished.

On another night, after closing hours, an employee heard chairs knocking against each other. When the employee investigated, the sound stopped. As soon as the employee started to walk away, the noise resumed.

The Spaghetti Warehouse may share a family of ghosts with the site of the Bitter End—and the romantic B-Side Bar—at 311 Colorado Street. The Bitter End location has many of its own ghosts as well, even before it was damaged by a terrible three-alarm fire in August 2005. Look for dark figures around the bar at the B-Side.

Not far from the Spaghetti Warehouse, and across the street from Oilcan Harry's (haunted by madam Blanche Dumont), Fado's Irish Pub at 214 West Fourth Street may have a ghost from when a theater occupied the site. Then again, it may be Celtic faeries who move the furniture, turn lights on and off, and move small objects.

And, Austin's ghosts are not just above ground.

According to local legend, underground tunnels and walkways connected city offices and respectable businesses with Austin's most popular brothels. Using these tunnels, men could visit their favorite prostitutes without being seen entering or exiting these "boarding houses."

Some Austin visitors report odd vibrations and sounds coming from beneath their feet, especially around the warehouse district.

Day or night, and above or below ground, downtown Austin may have more ghosts per block than any city in America.

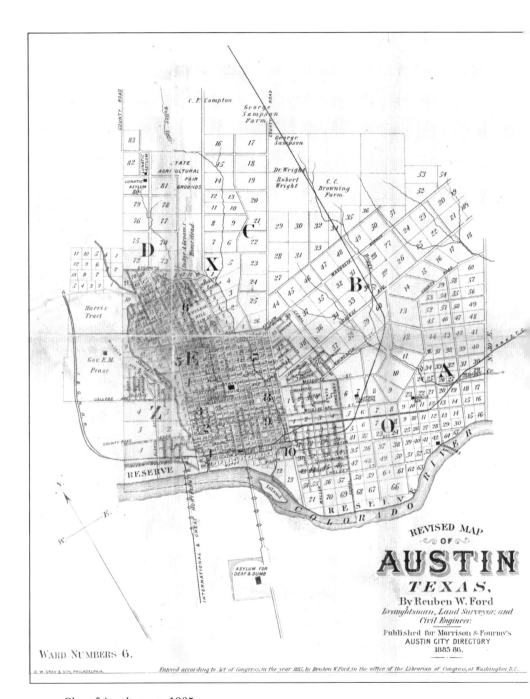

City of Austin map, 1885.

THE SHOAL CREEK CURSE

"It is a well-known tradition in Austin and vicinity that there is a buried treasure of great value on the banks of Shoal Creek, about a mile west of the city ..."

That's what famous storyteller O. Henry wrote in the 1890s when he and his friends were searching for treasure along the haunted shores of Shoal Creek. After a terrifying encounter one night, Henry and his friends swore never to return there again.

Like Gettysburg and Little Big Horn, Shoal Creek is so haunted that even the ground holds residual ghostly energy.

Before Europeans arrived in the Austin area, Native Americans lived and died at Shoal Creek. It was a source of water, limestone for cooking, and flint for arrowheads and sparking fires. In fact, hikers still find arrowheads around Shoal Creek. A path near the creek was once a Native American thoroughfare; today, it is the Shoal Creek Hike and Bike Trail.

Parts of Shoal Creek have always been sacred. A seven-foot tall Indian burial mound, covered in shale, was found near Old McCall Spring just west of Balcones Trail. Natives also revered the magic powers of Treaty Oak, at Shoal Creek just south of Duncan Park.

However, Shoal Creek is haunted for many more reasons than an ancient burial mound and a few Native legends. It has been the site of buried treasure, flash floods, and tragic deaths.

Buried Treasure and the Paymaster's Ghost

Where there is buried treasure, you'll find ghosts. Some are protecting the treasure while others are still looking for it.

Shoal Creek is home to at least two buried treasures. One of them is a cache of eighteenth century Spanish gold ingots, and the other is an 1836 Mexican payroll.

In the mid eighteenth century, one of the West's richest gold mines was in Digger Hollow, about fifteen miles northwest of Austin. Every day, burros carried heavy gold ingots from the mine to Mexico.

Then, early in 1770, the mine was hurriedly closed due to the threat of Indian attack. The manager of the mine ordered his men to hide seventy-five burro-loads of gold ingots in a cave. The entry was sealed, and the cave's location was marked on a flat rock that was hidden under a bush.

Then, the miners loaded eight burros with gold and headed towards Mexico. Their journey took them along the western border of Austin and the shores of Shoal Creek.

As they approached Barton Springs, the men realized that they were being followed. They quickly dug a hole and buried their gold. Soon after, Indians attacked, killing everyone except one small boy who hid in the bushes and told the tale later. The victims' bodies were left to rot on the shores of the Colorado River not far from Shoal Creek.

When nearby settlers discovered what had happened, they provided funerals and respectful burials for those who'd lost their lives, and the little boy was adopted by a local family.

According to one story, the gold was found many years later at Barton Springs. However, another story claims that the gold remains undiscovered somewhere near Shoal Creek, and the area is haunted by men who are still looking for it.

The second treasure has never been found. In 1836, a corrupt paymaster in Santa Anna's army stole the payroll. He buried it at Shoal Creek, but claimed that he had been ambushed. Soon after this, he was killed in a drunken brawl and never returned to recover the treasure.

Over the years, Shoal Creek has flooded many times and its landmarks have changed. It is said that on dark and moonless nights, the paymaster's ghost walks slowly along the creek. An eerie light from his spectral lantern has been seen as if it is floating in midair.

At about four a.m., I've seen this lamp bobbing along at about shoulder height. It flickers and moves unevenly not far from the bank of the creek.

Shoal Creek is also haunted by the ghosts of men whose lives were dedicated to—and destroyed by—their searches for Shoal Creek's treasure.

One of these ghosts is the gray, shadowy form of the Travis County Treasurer who, in 1896, embezzled $4,500 to buy a "correct chart" to the Shoal Creek treasure. He never received the map, and the money could not be replaced. When the state prepared to audit the Treasury accounts, the man committed suicide. A basically honest man, he is still searching Shoal Creek for the gold that would redeem his reputation.

Indian Raids and Failed Communities

No one knows how many people—Native Americans and settlers—died violent deaths at Shoal Creek. Records include the 1842 massacre of Gideon White, who'd lived at the artesian springs near Shoal Creek.

White left his log cabin one day to look for cattle, and was ambushed, probably by Comanches. The event has been described as a "terrible fight" during which White and others were killed.

Gideon White's grave is in Oakwood Cemetery. Psychics will find it quickly; the energy around it is very strange.

Some years later, Ed Seiders (pronounced like "Cedars") married Gideon White's daughter and they moved to the old White homestead. The spring was named after this family. Ed Seiders tried to create a resort at the springs, carving baths out of the limestone for which Shoal Creek is famous.

After a few years, Seiders sold the property to a developer who planned to build a subdivision on the land. However, that dream was swept away by Shoal Creek during the 1900 flood.

The shores of Shoal Creek have remained largely uninhabitable, despite repeated attempts to develop the land. Many say that the land is indeed cursed.

However, Ed Seiders is among the ghosts who are reported at the site. He's in good company among the spirits who return there to enjoy the baths he'd created during his lifetime.

Unmarked Graves

In addition to burial mounds, the unmarked graves of Native Americans and victims of Indian attack, Shoal Creek has been the site of many other burials.

During the Civil War, General Robert E. Lee camped by Shoal Springs when disease killed many of his men. Cholera epidemics were frequent in those years. No one knows how many of Lee's men were hastily buried at Shoal Creek, in an attempt to contain the fatal disease.

After the Civil War, General George Armstrong Custer arrived in Austin to enforce Reconstruction. He used the shores of Shoal Creek as a tent city for his soldiers. He also set up areas that he called bullpens, for unreconstructed Confederates.

During Custer's years in Austin, cholera and yellow fever swept through the community many times. Bodies of dead soldiers and some of the Confederates were placed in unmarked graves along Shoal Creek.

In later years when Shoal Creek flooded, the corpses rose to the surface and floated downstream. The soldiers' bodies were removed from their graves and reinterred at Arlington National cemetery. However, many people believe that approximately thirty-five bodies still remain in unmarked graves along Shoal Creek.

It's interesting that the number is estimated at thirty-five. That is the same number of people who were killed during the April 1915 flash floods. As the Austin American Statesman reported, "Houses were washed away, cows, horses, chickens and other fowls were careening down swelled Shoal and Waller Creeks to join the human corpses that had gone swirling before them to the bosom of the Colorado."

Ghost hunters wonder if the thirty-five bodies in unmarked graves at Shoal Creek have extracted their revenge, or if they still haunt Austin on rainy nights.

At least one ghost dates to the 1915 flood. Firefighter Thomas Edward Quinn lost his life at Shoal Creek while attempting to rescue people from the fast-rising waters. His spirit also returns on rainy nights, and he may protect people from Shoal Creek's frequent floods.

Haunted Grounds and Ghost-Filled Buildings

While studying the many ghosts of Austin, Texas, a pattern became obvious. Haunted houses built by Abner Cook—including the Texas Governor's Mansion and the Neill-Cochran Museum—far outnumber haunted homes built by others.

Studying Abner Cook's life for clues, there was no tragedy or pattern of accidents associated with the building of these houses.

However, Abner Cook was a frugal man. One reason why he secured so many building contracts is because he was able to underbid his competitors. He could keep his bids low by supplying his own lumber and his own bricks.

The bricks came from Abner Cook's factory on the haunted shores of Shoal Creek. Ignorant of the residual ghostly energy stored there, Mr. Cook constructed homes with clay from Shoal Creek. They were destined to be haunted.

Woodlawn and the Ghosts of Pease Mansion

Woodlawn was among the first homes built with Shoal Creek bricks.

James B. Shaw was an Irishman who had graduated from the University of Dublin and moved to New Orleans. There he courted a lovely socialite, who seemed dazzled by his good looks and clever turn of phrase. Soon after announcing their engagement, Shaw was offered a job as Comptroller for the Texas Republic, and bought 200 acres of land at Shoal Creek for his new home. The house was built by Abner Cook and named Woodlawn.

Even before the house was completed, Shaw encountered the Shoal Creek curse. Without warning, his fiancée broke their engagement and promptly married someone else. However, with the work on Woodlawn well under way, Shaw told Abner Cook to complete the house as planned.

James Shaw moved into the house by himself. In time, he found someone else to marry, but the home's bad luck lingered. Shaw and his wife were the parents of a beautiful little girl, but she died at age two. Shaw's loss was compounded when his wife died just a few months later.

Shaw had endured enough of the Shoal Creek curse. He moved to Galveston and sold Woodlawn to Elisha M. Pease.

Notes from the Other Side

James Shaw has dark eyes that glitter when he grins, and he's often laughing, even when the tale involves misfortune. Very little can dampen his spirits... no pun intended.

Shaw is a talkative spirit with a story to tell. He wants to say that he never felt that the house was wholly to blame for what happened with his New Orleans fiancée, or later events. And, whether the house was cursed or not, Mr. Shaw doesn't think that it got the best of him.

The two words that he'd use to describe his approach to life's adventures are "tenacity" and "cunning."

He admits that he was dealt some difficult cards, and there were tragedies in his life. However, he has no regrets, he's met up with his loved ones on the other side, and even resolved his differences with the ex-fiancée.

The Return of the Woodlawn Curse

What happened next may have been more malicious energy from the Woodlawn curse, or the result of a hasty decision during difficult times.

When General George Armstrong Custer arrived in Austin, Elisha Pease—now Governor Pease—was in Connecticut. Custer announced his intentions to use Woodlawn for his headquarters and as an infirmary for his men if necessary. Pease objected, and the house remained empty.

Instead, Custer moved into the abandoned Texas Institute for the Blind. This was another brick home built by Abner Cook using clay from Shoal Creek.

Unfortunately, the in-town location kept Custer at a considerable distance from his cavalry camped at Shoal Creek. Soon, disease swept through Custer's soldiers. Neill house—today known as the Neill-Cochran Museum—was used as a military hospital for the sick and dying men. Abner Cook had also built that house of bricks.

Governor Pease returned to Woodlawn and lived there with his family for many years, but the Shoal Creek curse wasn't finished with him. In 1883, Governor Pease died after a freak riding accident along the banks of Shoal Creek.

Pease Monument at Oakwood Cemetery. *Photo by the author.*

Pease's descendants owned Woodlawn until the mid-twentieth century when it was sold to Governor Allen Shivers. After Shivers and his wife died, Woodlawn became the property of the University of Texas, which promptly sold the house to the state. Before long, the state realized that they didn't want it either. The mansion is now privately owned.

According to Austin ghost lore, Custer's soldiers blamed Governor Pease for closing Woodlawn. If General Custer had moved into Woodlawn as planned, he might have identified the cholera problem sooner and isolated the contagious men.

Each year around the anniversary of the cholera outbreak, blue uniformed ghosts have been seen gazing solemnly from the banks of Shoal Creek towards Pease Mansion.

Right:
Elisha M. Pease's grave at Oakwood Cemetery.

I've seen the ghostly campfires of Custer's (or perhaps Lee's) soldiers. Three of them appeared as clearly as if they were real. In fact, when I spotted them from the road, I drove into the park to see if they were real or spectral.

I found plenty of orbs, but no lights of any kind and no evidence that anyone else had been in the park recently.

A Modern Haunting at Shoal Creek

In recent years, people have reported the ghost of a speed walker on Lamar Boulevard between 24th Street and 34th Street. She appears at about two a.m. in the morning, and wears a white cap, a white sweater, white leggings, and pink running shorts. According to the story, she worked late at night, and that's why she'd go walking at an odd hour. One night, she was struck by a car and killed. Since then, she haunts the route that she used to walk, and has been seen by many people.

Other Haunted Sites near Shoal Creek

Carrington's Bluff on David Street is a lovely 1877 home styled as an English country house. From the relaxing patio of this bed-and-breakfast, guests are in an ideal location to see the eerie, floating light from the ghost of the Mexican paymaster. (However, you can see the lights from many spots along David Street.)

Local ghost lore also claims that Carrington's Bluff's has its own ghost that turns a television on and off. And, a guest reported that he'd been visited in the shower by a helpful spirit who lent a hand as he washed his hair.

Notes from the Other Side

In a spiritual reading, the Carrington's Bluff ghost—who wants to be called Oliver—claims that he lived a mediocre life until he came into money before reaching middle age. He remained single, and spent the rest of his life enjoying a delightfully decadent and self-indulgent lifestyle. He died before the money ran out, thank heavens, and continues to have fun as he dances between this world and the other side. He takes great delight, even pride, in being as unpredictable as a ghost as he was during his life on earth.

Visitor's information

Ghost hunting is just one reason to visit Shoal Creek.

Shoal Creek offers over three miles of great trails for easy hiking and biking. Look for arrowheads as you stroll along the banks of the creek, or—if you're at Pease Park—you may find fossils in the Georgetown limestone.

The Shoal Creek Greenbelt follows the path of Shoal Creek, and includes over seventy-five acres of recreational land. It's part of the Austin Parks and Recreation Department.

Parking is available at the Shoal Creek Greenbelt near the 2600 - 2800 blocks of Lamar, and picnic tables make this a perfect late-afternoon destination. Pack some sandwiches and cool drinks, and enjoy the landscape while waiting for the ghosts to manifest.

Right:
The grave of Abner Cook, whose
buildings are often haunted.
Photo by the author.

THE TEXAS GOVERNOR'S MANSION

So many people haunt the Governor's Mansion, it's amazing that anyone can live there. Both upstairs and down, indoors and out, almost every corner of the mansion is haunted.

The oldest ghost may be Sam Houston's. According to legend, he haunts because he wasn't allowed to finish his term of office as Governor.

Sam Houston

During the Civil War, Houston refused to sign an oath of allegiance to the Confederacy.

At the time, he said, "To secede from the Union and set up another government would cause war. If you go to war with the United States, you will never conquer her, as she has the money and the men. If she does not whip you by guns, powder, and steel, she will starve you to death. It will take the flower of the country—the young men.

Sam Houston's home in 1837.

"In the name of the constitution of Texas, which has been trampled upon, I refuse to take this oath. I love Texas too well to bring civil strife and bloodshed upon her."

In 1861, when his political office required him to support the Confederacy, Houston refused. On March 16, 1861, he was evicted from the office of Governor.

Although President Lincoln offered Sam Houston 50,000 troops to defend his position as Governor, Houston declined, and, in 1862, quietly moved back to his home in Huntsville, Texas.

Houston's health declined quickly, and he died of pneumonia on July 26th, 1863.

He regularly visits the Governor's Mansion, especially the Sam Houston bedroom. That is the Southeast bedroom, which includes a bust of Houston as well as a hand-painted photo of him.

When you tour the Governor's Mansion, you'll also see some of his documents and letters. The room also contains the four-poster mahogany canopy bed that Houston bought in 1859.

Be sure to study the quilt on his bed. His ghost sits there. An imprint in the quilt usually marks Sam Houston's presence, and visitors can hear his audible sighs.

If you see Sam Houston in or around the Governor's Mansion, he can be identified by his unusual height. He was at least six feet tall, and some estimated his height at six and a half feet.

Some claim that, aside from his period clothing, Sam Houston's ghost bears a striking resemblance to the spirit of young Lyndon Baines Johnson, whose ghost revisits the Driskill Hotel in nearby downtown Austin.

Portrait of Sam Houston, 1858.

Notes from the other side

Sam Houston is proud to be remembered as a generous man. In life, he was dazzled by a witty and artistic woman. This probably refers to his long-time mistress, Pamelia Mann. She's the madam who haunts the ladies' rooms at Market Square businesses in downtown Houston, Texas.

Sam Houston claims that he's not ready for any afterlife that includes his third (and final) wife, Margaret Moffette Lea. In life, she "reformed" him, made him stop drinking, and join the Baptist church.

Sam Houston's Grave, Texas State Cemetery.

The Governor's nephew

The Mansion's second most famous ghost—and certainly its noisiest—is the nineteen-year-old nephew of Governor Pendleton Murrah. The nephew was a Confederate soldier, and may have been one of the troops who prevented a Union invasion in east Texas during the early months of 1864.

He visited Governor Murrah's family and fell in love with his cousin, who was also the Governor's guest at that time. When she didn't take the nephew's ardor seriously, he closed himself in the north bedroom. Shortly after midnight, he committed suicide with a pistol.

Since that terrible night in April 1864, the Mansion's residents and staff have heard mysterious footsteps, groans, and other strange noises coming from that room. Until the home was remodeled in 1925, the room was always kept locked.

Today, the bedroom remains open. However, it is in an upstairs area that is not open to the public.

Notes from the Other Side

Pendleton Murrah's nephew still obsesses about his failed romance. He regards himself as a great catch because of his family's wealth. He is aware that he may have acted rashly when he committed suicide. However, he seems to think that he had the last word, and sees his suicide as something positive, even a victory.

He's one of many ghosts who are unlikely to move on in any hurry. He likes the sympathy that he gets when this story is told. In fact, he's quite pleased with himself and will probably remain at the Governor's Mansion, continuing to make noise and get attention.

Pendleton Murrah

Pendleton Murrah may also haunt the Governor's Mansion. His life did not end the way that he intended it to.

Murrah was born in South Carolina in 1824, and was the son of Peggy Murrah, a single mother. Pendleton seemed to be a high achiever from an early age, and eventually attended Brown University in Rhode Island where he studied law.

Although Murrah was admitted to the Alabama bar, he set up his legal practice to Texas to become more active in politics. A staunch Confederate, he was easily elected as Governor of Texas after serving successfully in the state legislature. However, his term as Governor was more challenging than he expected. Law and order were difficult to maintain since most of the adult men were fighting in the war. In addition, the work force was greatly diminished, and Texas's economy suffered badly.

At the conclusion of civil war, Murrah believed that he was going to be arrested by arriving Union soldiers. One day in June 1865, the Governor locked his office, climbed on a mule and rode south to Mexico. He didn't even tell his wife, Susie, that he was leaving.

Two months later, Murrah was dead in Monterey, Mexico.

His ghost may be responsible for the doorknobs that seem to turn on their own. He wanders the Governor's Mansion, afraid to open doors in case Union soldiers might be on the other side.

Notes from the Other Side

Pendleton Murrah still dwells on his financial mistakes. He's not ready to move on because he is still learning important things. That may be true, but he seems to obsess about finding out who betrayed him—especially financially—and why. As long as he believes that he's a victim of others' choices, he'll probably continue to haunt the Governor's Mansion.

The Household Staff

Among the many male ghosts, at least one young woman manifests. She may be a former maid who was dismissed when she became pregnant in the late 1880s. She is sometimes heard sobbing quietly just outside the Governor's Mansion.

Texas Governor's Mansion in 1911.

Notes from the Other Side

There are several spirits among the Governor's Mansion's ghostly staff. Many of them go about their work daily, and are as unobtrusive after death as they were in life.

One maid left home too soon, and too naïve. On the road, she met a wonderful man who protected her from harm. He was courageous and handsome, and had brown hair and brown eyes. She does not say how involved she was with this man, or what happened to him. However, she seems to be waiting for him.

I suspect that he went to war and didn't return. Or, he may not have realized that this little maid expected him to remain in her life.

She is generally content to wait at the Governor's Mansion.

A married couple also remains at the mansion. They're young-in their late twenties or early thirties, and have well-defined goals. I think that they died in an explosion of some kind; it was a sudden death for both of them. They remain at the mansion, certain that they're saving enough from their wages to be able to buy a small farm and raise a family, later on.

The sobbing maid is not willing to share her story.

It's difficult to communicate with some spirits when a location has multiple hauntings. The ghosts look more real to each other than we do. Because there are so many of them at the mansion, they don't see any reason to cross over, and may not realize that they're dead.

Visitor Information

The Governor's Mansion of Texas is at the corner of 10th and Colorado Streets, near the Capitol building. Abner Cook built the brick mansion in 1856. The buff-colored bricks are their natural color; they came from a clay pit on the Colorado River.

You can tour the Governor's Mansion at 1010 Colorado Street most weekday mornings. For reservations (recommended) and a daily tour schedule update, call 512-463-5516.

Blackbird sitting atop a crypt.
Photo by the author.

MORE GHOSTS AROUND AUSTIN

The Texas Capitol

At least two ghosts haunt the Capitol building in Austin, and both are seen in broad daylight.

The most dramatic Capitol ghost is former Governor Edmund Jackson Davis, who ran for reelection in December 1873, but was defeated by a vote of two to one after a heated and controversial campaign.

By mid-January 1874, Davis had declared the election illegal and refused to leave the Capitol building. He took control of the lower floor of the building and surrounded himself with state police while his opponents—including the new governor—occupied the second floor.

The dispute ended when Davis' appeals to President Ulysses S. Grant for military support were denied. Davis was removed from office and reluctantly resigned.

Today, Governor Davis still haunts his old offices, looking sadly out of a window or gazing off into space as if badly confused. Others hear his footsteps, and odd rattling noises around the first floor of the Capitol.

He's also seen on the Capitol grounds on misty and slightly rainy days, especially in mid-winter. When Davis appears on the paved paths around the Capitol, he's a tall man with a beard and flowing moustache. Most people comment on his icy glare. Sometimes, he stands stock still and waits for people to pass, before resuming his walk. At other times, he appears lost in thought and seems to be pacing rather than actually going anywhere.

Texas State Capitol, 1907.

The other ghost at the Capitol is Robert Marshall Love. On a sunny June morning in 1903, when Love was State Comptroller, he was shot at his desk by W. G. Hill, a former employee. Mortally wounded, the amazed Love looked up and said to onlookers, "I have no idea why he shot me. May the Lord bless him and forgive him. I cannot say more."

Love's image has been captured by the many security cameras that surround the Capitol. His ghost is frequently reported by visitors who describe him as someone who's "dressed funny" and usually appears around the second floor of the Capitol building. People don't usually realize that he's a ghost until he vanishes, walking through walls.

Home Depot

Some spirits of women haunt the houses where they
lived, and can often be found enjoying their gardens. They
frequently visit hotels, cafes, restaurants, pubs, and bars
that remind them of happy memories.

Nineteenth century madams haunt the sites of their
brothels. These are the places where they enjoyed
popularity, a sense of power, and financial rewards.

So, it's perfectly reasonable that men would haunt the
locations where they've been happiest, even if that's a
hardware or DIY store.

Austin's Home Depot store at Brodie Lane by U. S. 290
is a favorite spot for several male ghosts.

One ghost is referred to as Fred. He may be a past
customer. He may be a visitor from a nearby cemetery.
His clothing can seem a little formal or out of date for the
store, but people are likely to mistake him for an employee,
even without the orange apron. If you see him, feel free
to ask him for advice about home repairs. He likes to feel
useful.

Another ghost at Home Depot is named Herb. He was
a craftsman kind of carpenter and enjoyed making things
for other people. If you see him in the store, he's likely to

be a jolly man with a sparkling blue eyes. If you ask him for directions in the store, he'll offer to show you the exact aisle that you need. However, he's a very fast walker and keeping up with him can be a challenge. Like Fred, this is a friendly ghost and you have no reason to be afraid of him. In fact, most people don't realize that he's a ghost at all.

There is also a cemetery behind Home Depot, on the west side of Brodie Lane. (For more information, see the Haunted Austin Cemeteries in Chapter Three.)

Central Market

Austin's Central Market is a popular grocery store for people who want the highest quality food. It's also popular with a few ghosts. No one is certain where these ghosts come from. They could be visitors from haunted Shoal Creek, just a few blocks away. Another rumor suggests that a late nineteenth century cemetery used to be in that vicinity. Others claim that the ghosts are amateur chefs who revisit one of their favorite shopping sites.

When interviewed, members of the Central Market staff claimed that the store is not haunted. They were reluctant to comment about the store's parking lot, where elevated EMF levels appear in the early morning hours.

Look for the Central Market at 38th Street and Lamar, just past Guadalupe. It's on the north side of downtown Austin.

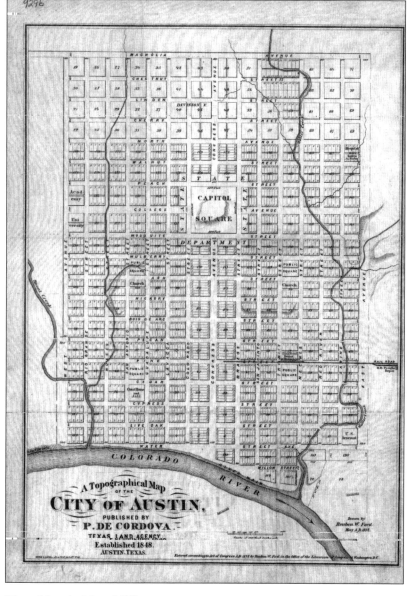

City of Austin Map, 1872.

Kleberg Stage

Ghost hunters know that almost every theater with a stage is haunted. From Broadway to college campuses, if there's a stage, there's probably a stagehand that haunts it. Likewise, there's almost always a ghost watching rehearsals from the back of the hall or a seat in the balcony.

The Kleberg Stage at 1510 Toomey Road at West Lamar Street fits this classic profile. Its ghosts are described as "annoying" as they move objects about, change the lighting, and hide props. At least one ghost is infamous for taking the actors' personal possessions and returning them some time later.

The infrequent ghost at the back of the hall usually manifests as a smoker. Despite no-smoking regulations, cast and crew can detect the aroma of cigarettes near the back row immediately after a rehearsal.

Paramount Theater for the Performing Arts

The Paramount Theater dates back to 1915, and it has been remodeled at least twice since then. Today, the theater is famous for high-quality movies and occasional live performances. Be sure to visit this Congress Street landmark, and watch for unusual lights near the projection booth. That's where staff have reported evidence of ghosts.

Northcross Mall

This mall hosts the annual Mansion of Terror haunted house attraction in October. And, it's scary enough to build considerable residual energy each year. Now, a few people have noted orbs around the mall after dark. In true "Conjuring Up Philip" form, the haunted house could be attracting spirits who want to help provide a "good scare."

Northcross Mall is at 2525 West Anderson Lane at Burnet Road, north of downtown Austin. You can take I-35 to Route 183 North, or use the MoPac Expressway and exit at Anderson Lane.

St. Julia's Catholic Church Grotto

It may not be haunted, but this location has astonishing spiritual energy. You'll enjoy the church's lovely gardens, but your destination is past it, in the little grotto featuring the Virgen de San Juan de Los Lagos amid flickering devotional candles. After dark, the view is especially memorable. You'll be glad that you brought your camera. It's thoughtful to leave a small donation for the shrine's upkeep, too.

The church is on the east side of Austin, not far from Austin Community College—Eastview. The street address is 3010 Lyons Road, between Pleasant Valley Road and Tillery Street.

Waters Park Road

Waters Park, sometimes called Watters, was a late nineteenth century settlement with a post office and a one-room schoolhouse. In the early twentieth century, it was a popular destination thanks to a resort built by the railroad, and nearby Seiders Springs (at Shoal Creek) and Hyde Park. When World War I began, tourists stopped flocking to this area, and families began to move away.

Little is left of the settlement except the road bearing its name. Waters Park Road runs parallel to the North MoPac Expressway, near West Parmer Lane, not far from Balcones District Park.

Ghost hunters recommend this area, especially around the large blocks of pink granite near West Parmer Lane. Those blocks are reminders of when a narrow-gauge line carried the granite from Granite Mountain near Burnet, to Austin where it was used in buildings. The railroad tracks turned sharply, and cars sometimes tumbled off. According to local lore, these accidents sometimes resulted in deaths, and this explains the supernatural activity in the area, including unexplained fog banks (perhaps ectoplasm) near the tracks.

51st Street & Manor Road and the Hornsby Family Cemetery

In northeast Austin, at 51st Street and Manor Road near Bartholomew District Park, look for a monument marking the site where Comanches shot and scalped Josiah Pugh Wilbarger. It's at the site of the old one-room schoolhouse once called Pecan Springs School.

Old schools are often haunted, but there's a darker reason why people photograph orbs and capture EVP at this site. Two unmarked graves may be there, from an 1833 massacre.

Josiah Pugh Wilbarger was born in Kentucky in 1801. He was the oldest of eight children. Wilbarger's first career was teaching. In Texas, after he married, he became a scout and a surveyor for Stephen Austin.

Right:
The Scalping of Josiah Wilbarger.

On a sultry August day in 1883, Wilbarger went scouting with four friends, Christian, Haynie, Standifer, and Strother. The five were surveying land north and east of present-day Austin. At noon, they paused for lunch and were attacked by about fifty Comanche Indians.

Haynie and William Standifer dashed to their horses and escaped successfully. However, Wilbarger was struck with arrows in both legs, took a bullet in the hip, and another through the throat. The Comanches scalped him and slit the throats of Thomas Christian and William Strother. Then, the Indians stripped their victims before leaving them for dead, and riding off with their horses.

Meanwhile, Haynie and Standifer rode to the nearest house, which belonged to Reuben and Sarah Morrison Hornsby and their eight children. Hornsby sent messages to his neighbors, and a group prepared to ride out in the morning to retrieve the bodies of the three fallen surveyors.

However, during the night, Sarah Hornsby had a dream in which Josiah Wilbarger was alive, leaning naked against a tree. She woke her husband to tell him about her dream, and described the tree in detail.

Right:
Reuben Hornsby, whose wife had the prophetic dream.

Mr. Hornsby did not take his wife's dream seriously. Comanches never left anyone alive after one of their raids. However, he agreed to bring Wilbarger back to the Hornsby home in the unlikely event that he was still alive.

The party rode to the scene of the massacre. They found the bloody, naked corpses of Christian and Strother and covered them each with a sheet. Then, Joseph Rogers spotted a figure leaning by a tree, naked and covered in what he thought was red war paint.

It was Wilbarger, standing exactly as Sarah Hornsby had described. Drenched in his own blood, with his skull exposed and dried from the heat of the relentless sun, Wilbarger had survived.

When Josiah Wilbarger told the story during the next few days, he remarked that his sister, Margaret Clifton, had appeared to him during the long night after his attack. She told him to rest and that help would arrive the next day. Then, she vanished as she walked in the direction of the Hornsby home.

Josiah knew that he must be delirious; Margaret lived more than 700 miles away, near St. Louis. She had never even visited Texas. How could she have found him?

Six weeks after he was scalped, Josiah learned that his sister, Margaret, had died the day before he was attacked.

When Wilbarger recalled the Comanches ripping his scalp off in silver dollar-sized pieces, he said that it "sounded like the pealing of loud, distant thunder."

Wilbarger became the father of five children and lived another eleven years. He died after a head injury inflamed what was left of his scalp bone. He and his wife, Margaret, are buried at the State Cemetery in Austin.

Wilbarger County was created and named for Josiah Wilbarger and his brother, Mathias.

The Hornsby family farm, where Wilbarger recovered from the Comanche attack, was six miles east of Austin. Today, a marker describes the history of the site, and says, "Here Josiah Wilbarger recovered after being scalped in 1833."

The scalping is one of Texas' best-documented legends, and among its most gruesome tales.

The Hornsby family cemetery is at the foot of the hill, next to where the farmhouse once stood. Rogers Hornsby, who is in the Baseball Hall of Fame, was Reuben Hornsby's great-great grandson. The famous baseball player's 1963 grave is also at this cemetery.

From Austin, take 19th Street east. After it crosses the Colorado River, it becomes FM 969. Follow it about nine miles to Hornsby Bend. Signs on FM 969 indicate the cemetery and marker.

It has no reported ghost stories, though several gruesome killings took place at Hornsby's Bend. There should be considerable ghostly activity at this location.

In 1836, two men named Haggett and Williams were killed by Indians in front of Reuben Hornsby's home.

Later that year, two more men—names unknown—were butchered by Indians at Hornsby's Bend. The two men were scalped, their arms cut off, and their hearts were eaten by their attackers.

In 1845, Daniel Hornsby and William Adkisson were fishing from Blue Bluff, about two minutes' walk from the Hornsby family cemetery. They were attacked from behind and killed by Indians.

In late 1892, ex-Sheriff Malcolm Morrison Hornsby was shot through the chest by belligerent visitors near the Hornsby home. He died shortly after the shooting.

Any site with this much rich history and violence is likely to hold considerable residual energy. In addition, a family so committed to the land and their home on it, is likely to revisit the site.

University of Texas

The University of Texas at Austin has some of the most interesting hauntings in Texas. As you'd expect, Littlefield House, the Music Building, and Jester Auditorium each have their own ghosts. This is typical of most universities, where dorms and theaters often report hauntings.

However, the most remarkable haunted building is the famous UT Tower, with eerie roots in the Shoal Creek Curse and the ghost of an English poet.

The original "Old Main" building at the University of Texas at Austin was built on a fifty-foot hill called College Hill. It was the final project of Abner Cook, whose houses are among Austin's most haunted. The majority of them were built with bricks that carry the Shoal Creek Curse.

University of Texas at Austin, 1902.

However, Cook's haunted bricks weren't the only eerie element at Old Main. The original building was accented with ivy taken from the Stokes Poges (England) grave of poet Thomas Gray (1716 - 1771). Some have seen this sad poet in his flowing academic robes, walking near the UT Tower building.

In the 1930s, Old Main was torn down despite protests, and replaced with the current building that includes the 307-foot-tall UT Tower. The ivy was replanted, and some of Abner Cook's original bricks were reused for the building, including the cornerstone.

Right:
UT Tower, completed.

One sultry summer day approximately thirty years later, twenty-five-year-old ex-Marine Charles Whitman climbed to the observation deck of the Tower, and began shooting. By the time Whitman was stopped by the Austin Police and DPS Officers' bullets, the ex-Marine had shot nearly fifty people, wounding fourteen of them fatally. The date was August 1, 1966, and its anniversary is still a dark day in Austin's history.

Charles Whitman is one of the ghosts who haunts the UT Tower today. He's sometimes seen as an odd, vanishing shadow. At other times, he appears as a faint figure in workmen's clothes, in or near the UT Tower. At night, when the building is empty except for security guards, Whitman's ghost turns on the lights until the guards ask him to stop.

In recent years, the observation deck has been extensively remodeled and is now open to the public. Tours are available by reservations, through the Texas Union Information Center.

Thomas Gray, whose graveside ivy was planted at the UT Tower site almost ninety years before the shootings, wrote these eerie words:

> *Alas, regardless of their doom,*
> *The little victims play!*

He could have been writing about the UT students who—thinking that the gunfire was just firecrackers—were shot by Charles Whitman. It's enough to give anyone chills.

CHAPTER TWO:
STRONG-WILLED SPIRITS—
FAMOUS PEOPLE
WHO HAUNT AUSTIN

SUSANNAH WILKERSON DICKINSON

Two guests emerged from downtown Austin's Hilton Hotel on a foggy March evening.

"Did you see what that woman was wearing?" one asked.

"Yeah, I'd love a Victorian gown like that. Put a black pointy hat with it, and she could be a witch for Halloween."

"Did you see where she went? It's like she vanished. "

"You're right," her companion agreed, pulling her sweater more tightly around her. "That was weird. It must be foggier than it looks."

Once again, Susannah Wilkerson Dickinson had visited the home where she was happiest during her extraordinary and colorful life. It's located across the street from the Hilton.

Like many girls born in Tennessee in 1814, Susannah Wilkerson never learned to read or write. She couldn't read the newspapers that put her name in the headlines, she didn't keep a diary, and she couldn't write her life story. We have to rely on others' tales of her… and what she shares from the other side.

Susannah's adventures began the day before her best friend's wedding. The groom, Almeron Dickinson, drove his carriage to Susannah's home, expecting to take her to his fiancée's home.

Fifteen-year-old Susannah had other ideas. The couple stopped in Bolivar, Tennessee, and were married that afternoon by a justice of the peace. Within two years, the couple had moved to Gonzales, Texas, where Almeron hoped to earn a comfortable living as a blacksmith.

Instead, after the Texas war of independence was sparked in Gonzales, Almeron volunteered as a soldier in the fight against Mexico. After several months at the Alamo, Almeron missed Susannah and his new daughter and asked them to move closer.

Susannah had barely arrived at a friend's home in San Antonio (then called Bexar), when the Mexican army was spotted nearby. Colonel William Travis ordered everyone into the Alamo for safety. Susannah hid with her daughter in the dark and smoky Alamo chapel, listening to gunfire and screaming outside its walls.

Historic marker at the grave of Susannah Wilkerson Dickinson in Oakwood Cemetery. *Photo by the author.*

Now and then, a mortally wounded soldier stumbled into the chapel, pleading for help or at least God's mercy. Susannah drew herself even further into the shadows, grateful that her daughter could sleep through this horror.

When the battle was over, twenty-two-year-old Susannah was the only adult Anglo to leave the Alamo alive. It was the beginning of a tumultuous life. During much of it, Susannah seemed to be pursued by her own ghosts.

About a year and a half after leaving the Alamo, Susannah married John Williams, but divorced him four months later.

Nine months after that, she married Francis P. Herring. In less than three years, he was dead.

Four years after Mr. Herring departed this world, Susannah married Peter Bellows and they moved to Houston. According to the divorce papers that Bellows filed in 1857, Susannah got the "seven year itch," she went to work at Mansion House and never returned home.

Mansion House was the most successful hotel and brothel in downtown Houston, owned by the famous madam and flamboyant Texas socialite, Pamelia Mann.

If you visit Houston, be sure to look for the ghost of Mrs. Mann at Market Square. She's a regular visitor to ladies' rooms on that block. She looks like a regular bar, club, or restaurant patron, except that she's wearing an elegant white gown.

After the divorce, Susannah left Houston and moved to Lockhart where she set up her own boarding house. Before long, Susannah was married again. This time her husband was Joseph William Hannig, a German woodworker, sixteen years her junior. They may have seemed an odd couple, but Susannah had finally found love and contentment.

Susannah sold the land that she had been granted as an heir to an Alamo soldier. With that money she bought a house on Pine Street between Neches and Red River. In that home, Joseph began making furniture, and worked as an undertaker on the side.

When Joseph's businesses were successful, they moved to a larger two-story home on the more fashionable side of town.

Susannah Wilkerson Dickinson Williams Herring Bellows Hannig died in 1883, at age sixty-eight, and was buried in Austin's Oakwood Cemetery.

Graveside monument for Susannah Wilkerson Dickinson Hannig. *Photo by the author.*

A slab marks the grave of Susannah Dickinson Hannig, reminding visitors of her connection to the Alamo. *Photo by the author.*

Joseph remarried and moved to San Antonio, but when he died, he asked to be buried next to Susannah. It had truly been a love match.

No one is certain when Susannah started revisiting the little home on Pine Street—now Fifth Street—in downtown Austin. However, she has appeared as a young woman in a simple but colorful dress, and as a middle-aged woman in an elegant black silk gown.

Over the years, Susannah's home was converted to a restaurant, then closed, and finally moved across the street to its present location. Guests in neighboring hotels have seen floating orbs of light around the house, in addition to her elusive, ghostly figure.

Ghostly orbs float near the former home of Susannah Wilkerson Dickinson. Across the street, hotel guests have seen her ghost walking along the sidewalk as if she was still alive. *Photo by the author.*

Notes from the Other Side

In a reading, Susannah wanted to share a few things about her life.

Susannah always saw herself as someone with a tremendous amount to share. It was her energy that drew other people to her. Some of them were "lesser men," as Susannah likes to joke when she talks about several of her husbands and lovers.

At least one husband was genuinely abusive and it took her awhile—too long, in her opinion—to realize that he was angry with himself and with his own life, rather than anything that she did or didn't do. She wanted to help him, but finally realized that she couldn't.

At the Alamo, she's not sure why General Santa Anna let her live. She was afraid of him, but also so very exhausted from sleeplessness. She'd also been wounded in the leg, and a continuing stomach ailment was acting up. Santa Anna said that it was fine to leave, so she did, and put miles between her and the Alamo as quickly as she could.

Susannah is aware that her stories about the Alamo don't always fit together. She says that it's because the experience was like a dream, and—even now—she's not sure what really happened. She tried to block out a lot of it, and when others suggested parts of the story to her, those promptings seemed every bit as real as her surreal and broken memories.

If she'd been able to write, she might have written the events in a journal or diary to re-read and clarify later. Instead, she had to rely on memories and logic. But, she reminds us, the killing was senseless and so there is little logic to apply to what she remembers of the Alamo.

At the present time, Susannah is enjoying life on "the other side." It's another adventure for her, and one where the rules are very different.

She haunts her old home because it was the place where she spent her happiest years on earth. How she appears is related to the time that she's remembering, and how she is thinking of herself during that visitation.

Living with a much younger man, she often saw herself as twenty or more years younger than her calendar age. So, when she's recalling happy years with Mr. Hannig, she may look as if she's in her late twenties, and simply dressed.

At other times, she recalls being very aware of her maturity and responsibilities. When she's remembering that role, she's older. She's likely to wear black because, in connection with her husband's work as an undertaker, she was frequently called upon to console the bereaved.

After the house was moved to its current location, Susannah was especially anxious about it. She visits regularly to make sure that it's still okay.

Susannah also haunts because a loved one is missing. I'm pretty sure that it's someone male, and she hasn't found him yet. Perhaps he's been unwilling to cross over.

She's not sure what to think. It's not that she's miserable without him, but she frets about him and his well-being. For this reason, she searches this earthly plane for him, now and then, in case he's looking for her, too.

When she finds him and confirms that he's "in a suitable place," as she describes it, she'll probably be a less frequent visitor to the earthly plane.

Susannah's last husband, Mr. Hannig, also haunts Austin. He rarely appears, but when he does, it's usually at the top floor of the building that still bears his name, the Hannig Building. Look for his pale figure at the upstairs windows, as he looks over the street, especially late at night.

BEN THOMPSON, AUSTIN'S GHOSTLY GAMBLER AND SHERIFF

Gunslinger Ben Thompson just can't stay away from Austin. Even today, more than 125 years after his death, Ben continues to haunt the sites of his favorite saloons and brothels in downtown Austin.

Ben Thompson was born in 1843, in the English town of Knottingley, Yorkshire. He was the oldest of five children. His family moved to Austin when Ben was about seven years old, and his father took a job in a printing shop.

Long before Ben became known as a hired gun and professional gambler, his temper often got the best of him.

When he was only fourteen years old, Ben Thompson had already been convicted for wounding another young man with a shotgun. At age seventeen, Thompson killed a Frenchman in New Orleans in a knife duel.

When he was eighteen, he enlisted in the Confederate Second Regiment Texas Mounted Rifles where he shot and killed a fellow soldier. Shortly after that, he escaped from jail and joined Maximilian's forces. He spent two years in Mexico and returned to Austin where he married Catherine Moore, the daughter of an Irish immigrant, and then shot her brother James.

After many other adventures and misadventures, Ben Thompson met Philip Coe. Together, they opened the Bulls Head Tavern and Gambling Saloon in Abilene, Kansas. Coe was soon shot by Wild Bill Hickok—then called "Duckbill" Hickok because of his extended upper lip—and Thompson returned to Austin once again.

His next employer was the Atchison, Topeka and Santa Fe Railway, where he worked as a hired gun during a right-of-way dispute with another railway. This was settled peacefully, and Thompson was well rewarded as he returned to Austin yet again.

With his earnings, Thompson opened a gambling hall above the Iron Front Saloon at Pecan (later Sixth) Street and Congress Avenue in downtown Austin. It was a popular den of iniquity with gambling, loose women, and plenty of liquor.

Based on his popularity and reputation for honest tables, Ben Thompson ran for City Marshal, but lost the election to another saloon owner, Edward Creary.

Thompson had learned his lesson. According to one version of the story, when Creary prepared to run for reelection, Thompson shot him. Creary quickly withdrew. Thompson ran unopposed, but before the election, he shot and killed Mark Wilson and a bartender at Wilson's Senate Saloon and Variety Theatre.

Thompson was elected anyway.

For the next two years, Thompson stayed sober and did a good job as City Marshal of Austin. Only one murder was committed in the city; the victim was a horse thief shot during a struggle in Sallie Daggett's brothel.

The eerie grave of Sheriff Ben Thompson at Oakwood Cemetery. Note the ghostly, unexplained shaft of light directly above his headstone. *Photo by the author.*

Because he brought law and order to Austin, Marshal Ben Thompson was admired and liked throughout the west. His friends included famous lawmen and gunfighters such as Doc Holliday and Wyatt Earp.

Speaking about Thompson, gunfighter Bat Masterson once said that he was doubtful "if in his time there was another man living who equaled him with a pistol in a life-and-death struggle."

But, in some parts of Texas, Thompson is still had enemies. One of them was Jack "Pegleg" Harris, a notorious San Antonio saloon owner.

Harris was described as a one-armed Confederate veteran with a quick wit and an equally quick temper. He didn't like Thompson, and said so often... and loudly. Harris offered a reward to anyone who would kill the Austin marshal, with the assurance of a "speedy trial and acquittal" if the shooting took place in San Antonio.

Finally in 1882, Marshall Ben Thompson boarded a train for San Antonio where he shot and killed Jack Harris. The jury decided that it was self-defense, but—after seven months in a San Antonio jail awaiting trial—Thompson's career as a lawman was over. He was forced to resign.

Ben Thompson planned to open another saloon and gambling house, but times had changed in Austin. During his time as City Marshal, Thompson had driven out too much of the wild element that provided business for his saloons. For the first time in his life, Ben Thompson was without a job.

Soon, Thompson was drinking again. He went to a play in Austin and, in the middle of it, started shooting at the actor who was playing the villain. According to some stories, Thompson's wife had loaded his gun with blanks. Others claimed that Thompson was too drunk to hit the broad side of a barn anyway.

In March 1884, Ben Thompson met his end back in San Antonio. No one is certain why he returned to that city, and especially to the saloon owned by Jack Harris' partner, Joe Foster. By many accounts, it was an ambush by Foster's hired gunmen.

Whether or not it was a fair fight, Ben Thompson was dead with nine bullets in him when the smoke cleared. The fatal shots had hit Thompson from behind. The jury declared it justifiable homicide.

Ben Thompson's body was brought back to Austin and buried in Oakwood Cemetery. His funeral cortege had included sixty-two carriages.

However, the story doesn't end there. Shortly after the funeral, people began noticing the crisp sound of Ben Thompson's boots and his distinctive cigar smoke at the Iron Front Saloon, when no one else was around.

In 1910, the Iron Front Saloon was torn down and replaced by the Littlefield Building, which soon became the city's financial center. However, Thompson's footsteps were still heard in the halls of the building, and continue to this day. His cigar smoke sometimes wafts through the smoke-free building. People also say that Ben Thompson's ghost is responsible for the "empty" elevators that operate themselves and travel to the top floor without any apparent occupants. And, if you hear the sound of boots walking nearby but don't see anyone, that's probably Sheriff Thompson making the rounds of his favorite saloon.

Notes from the Other Side

Ben Thompson is a charming but vain man who refuses to accept the finality of his death. He's still waiting to strike it rich with one of his gambling dens. He believes that an ace remains in his deck, and he enjoys the attention that he earns as a famous Austin ghost.

In terms of the twenty-first century—which he doesn't believe is the current time—Mr. Thompson would prefer to see himself represented as a gentleman in a suit and a top hat. Although he lived in the "Wild West" and earned a living as a hired gun, he does not think of himself as a rough-and-tumble cowboy.

Even more ghosts

Ben Thompson is just one of several ghosts at the Littlefield Building.

Major George Washington Littlefield was the man who owned and directed the construction of the Littlefield Building. In its day, this building was the tallest skyscraper between New Orleans and San Francisco. Major Littlefield is sometimes heard clearing his throat in the lobby and on the top floor of this building. He also looks out from that top floor. You can sometimes see his outline, or even a brief glimpse of his face, looking out of the third window from the left, at the top floor of the building along the Sixth Street side.

A woman who looks like Eleanor Roosevelt has also been seen at dusk, entering the lobby of the Littlefield Building. She's most often seen just inside the doors after the building has closed for the night.

Eleanor Roosevelt visited this building when Lyndon Baines Johnson—who later became America's thirty-sixth President—was the Texas state director of the National Youth Administration. She wanted to learn "why the Texas NYA director was doing such an effective job."

Others claim that the ghostly woman just inside the lobby doors is one of the female tellers whom Littlefield employed in the ladies banking department of his American National Bank.

American President Lyndon Baines Johnson may haunt the building as well, but he's more often sighted next door at the Driskill Hotel, where he used to watch election returns on television.

Whether the ghosts include LBJ or not, some people have seen faint, flickering lights through the sixth floor windows. During LBJ's tenure with the National Youth Administration, he was known for working late hours with his staff, and the offices were lit only by gas lamps after ten p.m.

Visit the Littlefield Building

The Littlefield Building is at the northeast corner of Sixth Street and Congress Avenue. Because it is a corner location, it has two addresses: 106 East Sixth Street and 601 Congress Street. It is on the same block as the haunted Driskill Hotel.

The Littlefield Building is usually open during normal business hours.

JACK THE RIPPER'S EARLY DAYS IN AUSTIN

Most of Austin's ghost stories are colorful. Austin ghost hunters enjoy talking about irreverent cowboys and eccentric cattle barons, generous hotel managers, salty-tongued madams, and independent-minded women like Susannah Dickinson, who stared down Santa Anna's men.

From its "Wild West" days to the occupation by General Custer's men, to the ghostly jogger near Shoal Creek, almost every chapter of Austin's ghostly history is interesting and fun.

Almost…but not entirely.

One very dark chapter left a brutal emotional gash on the city.

In the mid-1880s, Austin was the scene of attacks so grisly that most history books don't describe them. The truth is, Jack the Ripper may have started his killing spree in Austin.

Most people prefer not to talk about the gruesome murders that scarred downtown Austin. Empty lots and pavement are silent memorials at those murder sites. People simply don't want to build there, even when the neighborhoods are prime commercial real estate.

Whether they know about the murders—and the ghosts—or not, people unconsciously cross the street to avoid the powerful and ugly energy at many of these sites. If you're a psychic, you'll sense this almost immediately.

Bird's eye view of downtown Austin around 1890.

In 1884 and 1885, the Austin killer attacked as many as twenty people—mostly women—and slaughtered at least seven of them. He left Austin in January 1886. In 1888, Jack the Ripper killed five women in and near London's White Chapel district.

At first, the Austin killer attacked "servant girls." His last known Texas victim sometimes worked as a prostitute.

As the Austin Statesman newspaper reported on September 5, 1888:

> "There is a striking similarity… between these murderers across the water and the servant girl murderers in Austin in 1885, which latter remains a mystery as profound and unraveled as that of Whitechapel.
>
> "All were perpetrated in the same mysterious and impenetrable silence, and what makes the coincidence more singular is that the Austin murder fiend, who was seen on one occasion, was, like 'Leather Apron,' a short, heavy set personage."

In fact, there are several possible men who were in Austin during 1885 and in London during 1888. They include a doctor, an aristocrat, and a cook who worked at Austin's Pearl House hotel.

The Mystery of the Malay Cook

Most of the Austin murder victims were killed within a few blocks of Pearl House, a small railroad hotel at the southeast corner of Congress and Third Streets. Pearl House was later acknowledged as a "house of ill repute."

Pearl House employed a Malay cook between 1884 and January 1886. When the cook left Austin, the killings abruptly stopped. But, that's not the only evidence against him.

In 1888, the New York World newspaper reported:

"During the bloody butchery of women in this city three years ago there was a Malay cook at work in a cheap boarding-house in the vicinity of which two of the bloodiest of all the terrible assassinations occurred.

"On Christmas eve, 1885, two women were murdered and horribly cut and slashed. One was just two blocks from the boarding-house where the Malay cooked. He was strongly suspected and was shadowed by detectives for two or three days, when he suddenly disappeared..."

That cook was in London in 1888.

On October 8, 1888, the Irish Times newspaper reported,

"the Malay said he had been robbed by a woman of bad character, and that unless he found the woman and recovered his money he would murder and mutilate every Whitechapel woman he met."

During that conversation, the cook revealed the sharp, two-sided blade that he carried for that purpose.

In 1888, the Atchison Daily Globe reported:

"An article published in the Daily Statesman, calling attention to the similarity of the Austin and London crimes and especially the fact that a Malay cook running on ocean vessels was suspected, called forth a letter to the editor. The letter stated that a Malay cook had been employed at a small hotel in Austin in 1885, the date of the Austin assassinations.

"A reporter investigated the matter, calling on Mrs. Schmidt, who kept the Pearl House, near the foot of Congress Avenue opposite the Union depot, three years ago. It was ascertained that a Malay cook calling himself Maurice had been employed at the house in 1885 and that he left some time in January 1886.

"It will be remembered that the last of the series of Austin women murders was the killing of Mrs. Hancock and Mrs. Eula Phillips, the former occurring on Christmas eve 1885, just before the Malay departed, and that the series then ended. A strong presumption that the Malay was the murderer of the Austin women was created by the fact that all of them except two or three resided in the immediate neighborhood of the Pearl House.

"Mrs. Hancock and her husband, lived within one block, and so did Mary Ramie, the colored girl, and others who were assassinated in their beds and dragged out into their yards."

Was the Malay cook also Jack the Ripper? Evidence points in that direction.

America's First Serial Killer

The gruesome murders began at New Year's Eve in 1884, when the body of Mollie Smith, a servant girl, was found in the snow next to the outhouse behind 901 W. Pecan Street. The killer had cut a large hole in her head.

In May 1885, two more female servants—Eliza Shelley and Irene Cross—were butchered near downtown Austin. They were followed by a similar murder in August and two in September, taking the lives of little Mary Ramey, Grace Vance, and Orange Washington.

Newspaper clipping from the September 29, 1885 killings.

A COLORED TRAGEDY.

A Negro and His Mistress Murdered in North Austin, Tex.—Culprit Arrested.

AUSTIN, TEX., September 29.—About one or two o'clock yesterday morning, Mr. Dunham living in North Austin, heard a noise in his servants' cabin, back of his residence, as if some one had jumped through the window, followed by a woman screaming. Orange Washington and Gracie Vance, living with Washington as his wife, and two mulatto girls, Lucinda Boddy and Sofy Gibson occupied the cabin. Coming out with a gun Mr. Dunham found Lucida scuffling with a man at the gate and he might have shot him, had the girl not caught Mr. Dunham in her agony and fright in such a way as to unintentionally prevent his shooting. This resulted in the man's escaping, though a number of shots were fired at him by others. Washington was found senseless and soon died. The two girls were, as one of them says, knocked senseless with a sandbag. She thinks from his voice, as he ordered her to keep quiet, that Doc Woods was the man. Gracie Vance was found to have been dragged through the window, thrown over the fence and dragged some distance from the cabin, where evidence of a severe struggle indicated that she had probably been outraged and then beaten to death with a rock which was found near by besmeared with blood. A watch was found on her person with the chain tied around her arm. A horse was also found saddled and tied to a tree near the scene of the tragedy. These facts may lead to the identity of the murderer should Woods be the wrong man. His brother, Doug. Woods, has been arrested on suspicion of being accessory, if not principal in the murder; also Beverly Overton, another negro who owns the horse, but claims it was stolen from him. The police claim the watch had been stolen also. If so, it may have been tied to the arm as a device to fasten suspicion on the owner. Doc Woods was afterward arrested and identified by Lucinda Boddy as the criminal.

These early victims were usually servants in wealthy white homes. The killer was soon dubbed "the Servant Girl Annihilator" by Austin resident William Sydney Porter. (Porter is better known as short story author O. Henry.)

The citizens of Austin were shocked and demanded better law enforcement, but every arrest was a dead end.

It took awhile for the police to realize that this was the work of a single killer. Each attack was slightly different from the one before it. Was the Ripper practicing his craft?

Late in December 1885, the killer changed his pattern again. His last known Austin victims were two wealthy white women. Eula Phillips and Susan Hancock were found dead within hours of each other.

Mrs. Hancock had just returned home from a charity concert when she was butchered. Mrs. Phillips lived less than a mile away from her, in one of Austin's wealthiest neighborhoods.

Eula Phillips' death provides the strongest indication that the killer was Jack the Ripper, honing his skills in Austin: In the hearing that followed her death, evidence showed that the wealthy and celebrated Mrs. Phillips had amused herself by working as a prostitute at Delia Robinson's brothel.

Her husband was aware of this, and explained that he'd bought "chamomile flowers, extract of cottonwood and ergot" to end at least one of Eula's unwanted pregnancies.

After these two murders on Christmas Eve 1885, the killings in Austin stopped. Seven women and one man had lost their lives to America's first serial killer.

Despite eyewitnesses and the use of bloodhounds to track the scent, the Austin killer consistently eluded the police.

The Austin Statesman newspaper reported that the crimes were clearly conceived "...with a superior intelligence," noting that, "... brain work of a high order will have to be invoked to discover the perpetrators."

In a detective's notes published in 1910, Jack the Ripper was similarly described as, "possessing both shrewdness, caution, and intelligence."

To catch the Austin killer, or at least make it harder for him to commit his crimes undetected, unusual measures were necessary.

After the Christmas Eve murders in 1885, the City of Austin established patrols and interrogated everyone on the streets at night. Then, the City of Austin installed thirty-one "moonlight towers" to light the streets.

Austin's Moonlight Towers

The moonlight towers were purchased from the City of Detroit. Each one towered 150 feet above the street and used carbon arc lamps to cast light in a 3,000-foot circle. The company that installed them guaranteed that the light was bright enough to read a watch at night without squinting.

They are called "moonlight towers" because the light resembled very bright, blue moonlight.

Austin is the only city in the world known to use the moonlight towers today.

More than a dozen of them are still in use in Austin, and can be seen above the downtown. In 1936, the carbon arc lamps were replaced with mercury vapor lamps and an on/off switch at the base of each.

In 1970, the towers became an official state landmark. Since 1976, they are listed in the National Register of Historic Places.

Some of the easiest to spot are the lamps at West 4th Street and Nueces Street, not far from La Zona Rosa, and at West 9th Street and Guadalupe Street near the downtown Austin Public Library.

In the center of each tower, you can sometimes identify the small, hand-powered elevator that was used to repair the fixtures and replace light bulbs. With today's more modern lighting, the bulbs rarely need replacing.

Follow the Haunted Trail of Jack the Ripper in Austin

If you'd like to make a "Jack the Ripper Tour" of Austin, there are several locations to visit. Remember that many of the victims were chased or dragged from where they were first attacked. For the best results, ghost hunters should investigate the neighborhood around each murder site.

The following locations are approximate.

- **The Malay cook**—one of the most likely suspects— lived and worked at the Pearl House hotel. Today, the former Pearl House hotel building at 227 Congress Avenue hosts the nonprofit Latino arts organization La Peña. The Pearl Hotel's history as a brothel in the 1920s makes it a good candidate for hauntings, whether or not the Malay cook was a killer.

Special Note: If he was the murderer, his energy may linger for several blocks around the old Pearl House hotel location. It's never smart to go ghost hunting alone, but in this area, that's an especially strong warning. If you're also psychic, shield yourself well or avoid these sites altogether.

- **Mollie Smith** was killed near her home behind the William Hall residence at 901 West Pecan Street, now called Sixth Street. It's about three quarters of a mile from where Pearl House hotel was. In 2006, Mollie Smith's murder site was still an empty lot at the corner of Sixth Street and Bowie Street, about a block west of haunted Shoal Creek.

- **Eliza Shelley**'s body was found at the corner of San Jacinto Boulevard and Cypress Street. She was killed on May 6, 1885. Cypress Street is now Third Street. That murder site is about three blocks from the old Pearl House hotel.

- **Irene Cross** was found across from Scholz's Beer Garden at 1607 San Jacinto Boulevard. Today, that restaurant is often called Scholz Garten. Built in 1866, it's the oldest biergarten in Texas, and Austin's oldest restaurant. Any site with that much history is likely to have some ghosts and orbs, regardless of the events across the street.

- **Mary Ramey**—who was only eleven or twelve years old when she was murdered—lived with her mother Rebecca behind the home of Valentine O. Weed. Mary's name appears as "Masy" in some records. The address is alternately described as Trinity and Cypress (West Third) Street, or San Jacinto and Cedar Street (Fourth Street). Both are about a block from Eliza Shelley's house.

- **Gracie Vance** and her common law husband Orange Washington—the only known male victim of Austin's "Servant Girl Annihilator"— lived in a servants' cabin behind Major Dunham's house at Guadalupe Street near the university.

- **Susan Hancock** lived at San Jacinto Boulevard, and was found in a backyard on the south side of Water Street, a block east of Congress Avenue. Like Mary Ramey, a sharp, thin object had been inserted into her brain through her ear. Look for her ghost around 98 San Jacinto Boulevard; the closest landmark is the Four Seasons Hotel.

- **Eula Phillips** lived with her husband James O. Phillips and was found dead near her home on the corner of Hickory and Lavaca Streets. Hickory Street is now 8th Street, and the location is near the Austin Public Library at 800 Guadalupe Street, about a block from one of Austin's famous moonlight towers.

Do the Ripper's Victims Also Haunt Their Graves?

Many ghosts haunt the sites of their murders as well as their graves. Some also haunt the graves of their killers.

Most of the victims were buried in Oakwood Cemetery.

Eliza Shelley was thirty years old when she was killed in May 1885. She was buried four days later in the "colored ground" at Oakwood Cemetery.

Later that month, Irene Cross—described as "Irina Cross" in the cemetery records—was also buried in the colored ground at Oakwood Cemetery.

Mary Ramey's burial record gives her name as "Mary Ramy," an eleven-year-old who was buried on 31 Aug 1885, also in the colored ground at Oakwood Cemetery.

Grace Vance, age twenty-two and her common-law husband, Orange Washington (listed as O. Washington in the burial records) were interred in Oakwood's colored ground on September 29, 1885, two days after they were murdered.

Sue Hancock is listed as S. C. Hancock, a forty-four-year-old murder victim. She was buried on December 29th in Lot 459 at Oakwood Cemetery.

Eula Phillips' burial record says that she was eighteen years old, buried in Oakwood Cemetery's "old graveyard" on Christmas Day in 1885. She was a descendant of the "Old Three Hundred," the settlers who first received land grants in Steven Austin's Mexican colony. Her name is listed as Luly Philipps.

Oakwood Cemetery usually closes at dusk, and the cemetery is well patrolled to prevent vandalism.

However, that doesn't pose a problem for ghost hunters. An iron fence surrounds Oakwood Cemetery. It's not necessary to enter the cemetery to take photos of the graves after dark.

CHAPTER THREE:
GRAVE ENCOUNTERS— AUSTIN'S HAUNTED CEMETERIES

HAUNTED AUSTIN CEMETERIES

If you're looking for a reliably haunted place, start with an old cemetery. All that you need is a flash camera, and you can get remarkable evidence of hauntings... if the cemetery is old enough.

Many modern cemeteries are rarely haunted. There's no reason for the deceased to linger in these sterile locations. This generally includes cemeteries opened after the mid-twentieth century.

On the other hand, cemeteries from the nineteenth century and earlier are often haunted. There are a variety of reasons for this, including magnificent art on the unique headstones of that era. Ghosts seem to be drawn to visually unusual places.

Austin's cemeteries are some of the most beautiful in the United States. They are well worth visiting, whether you are a ghost enthusiast or not.

Left:
An open gate at an Oakwood Cemetery plot. *Photo by the author.*

One of many magnificent monuments at Oakwood Cemetery.
Photo by the author.

Many cemeteries within Austin's city limits are private and cannot be explored without permission. If you aren't sure if the cemetery is gated or locked, assume that it isn't open to the public. Research its ownership. Never trespass.

Austin's public cemeteries generally close at dusk, so you'll need permission to explore them after dark. Check with the police for access to city cemeteries at night. Most of them are well patrolled at night to prevent vandalism. When you see the quality of art on these headstones, you'll appreciate the police's efforts to secure Austin's extraordinary cemeteries.

Texas ghost hunters are especially lucky. Most Texas cemeteries are surrounded by iron bars or a chain link fence. It's not necessary to go inside these cemetery to take great ghost photos after dark.

Explore each cemetery during the day, when open. Many ghost hunters keep a journal to record the locations of important graves. Then, when you return to the site after dark, you'll know where to point your camera to capture spirit images near famous and haunted graves.

However, even in daylight, it can be difficult to read the information on some headstones.

Most historic Texas grave markers are carved from marble, limestone, or sandstone. These materials were used because they were relatively soft stone, and easier to carve by hand. However, that same softness has resulted in weather damage, and some stones are illegible as a result.

For awhile, genealogists and ghost hunters used shaving cream to illuminate the carvings. Then, we learned that the chemicals in these compounds could cause even more damage to the stones.

Instead, use a very bright flashlight. Angle it so that the carved areas are cast in shadows. Then, write down what you think you see on each headstone and marker. You can often compare your notes with cemetery records and other genealogical resources, if you're not sure whose grave is indicated.

Fortunately, granite markers and monuments have been used more often since the early twentieth century. They are harder and have fared much better.

Austin's three most famous cemeteries provide a variety of interesting sights for ghost enthusiasts.

Oakwood Cemetery

Oakwood Cemetery is large, ancient, and filled with beautiful gravestone art. From simple headstones to ordinate monuments and some crumbling crypts, Oakwood offers myriad opportunities for great photos.

Many of Austin's ghosts are represented in this cemetery. It is the oldest cemetery in Austin. Some of the most haunted graves are unmarked and next to the fence on Navasota Street. A second group of very haunted graves is on the opposite side of the cemetery, in the older sections.

If you're looking for a particular grave, you can use the City of Austin's online database of Oakwood Cemetery burial records. (At publication, the URL was http://www. ci.austin.tx.us/library/ahc/oakwood.htm.)

There are two related cemeteries: Oakwood Cemetery and Oakwood Annex Cemetery. Both are haunted, but the Annex is haunted for a more grisly reason.

Oakwood Annex Cemetery is across Navasota Street, facing Oakwood Cemetery. The Annex was added when Oakwood Cemetery filled. Most—but not all—of the Annex's graves are too new to be significantly haunted.

However, around 1900, medical school professors used cadavers to teach students in lecture halls. The primary sources for these bodies came from the stealing of dead bodies— usually paupers' cadavers stolen immediately before or after burial.

An empty, vandalized grave in Oakwood Cemetery. *Photo by the author.*

The problem became significant enough that, in 1913, Austin citizens demanded decent burial for paupers, and the city decided to use Oakwood Annex for this. Some hauntings may have resulted from desecrated graves, and indignities performed upon paupers' bodies.

Evergreen Cemetery,
3304 E 12th Street, at Airport Boulevard

A few graves at Evergreen Cemetery date back to the late nineteenth century, but most of more than 10,000 graves are from the twentieth century. Some histories say that the cemetery opened in 1928, and people reinterred their loved ones in this spacious cemetery. It's not clear how widespread that practice was. An adjoining cemetery, Highland Park Cemetery, became part of this city cemetery in the mid-twentieth century.

Texas State Cemetery, 909 Navasota Street

Austin's state cemetery is not far from Oakwood Cemetery and, during visiting hours, you can pick up a brochure for a self-guided tour. This site has been a cemetery since 1851, but most additions and improvements started in the twentieth century. You'll notice that many of the monuments and headstones showed death dates from before that time. In some cases, especially during a reinterment project between 1929 and 1936, these graves were moved from other cemeteries. Other monuments are simply tributes to the people represented on them; their actual graves remain elsewhere.

Most of the headstones and monuments bear the names of very famous people, from politicians such as John Connelly to author James Michener. The Father of Texas, Stephen Fuller Austin, was reinterred at the cemetery in 1910, and his monument is one of the most impressive.

The state cemetery's stunning displays include row after row of small, identical white headstones representing the graves of over 2,000 Confederate soldiers and their wives. Ghost hunters know that when people are buried in undistinguished graves, paranormal activity—especially EMF levels—tend to be higher than usual.

Like Oakwood Cemetery, the state cemetery closes at dusk. But, also like Oakwood and most other Texas cemeteries, you can take nighttime photographs from outside its walls, looking through openings in the fence.

Austin State Hospital Cemetery

The Austin State Hospital Cemetery is rich with history. Its locations may be worth visiting if you're a ghost hunter with nerves of steel. "Locations" is correct, because most of the bodies were reinterred at the current cemetery location. However, some bodies may remain at the old site near the main Austin State Hospital building at 4110 Guadalupe Street, once called Asylum Avenue.

The newer cemetery, which has a gated entrance at 51st Street, is the final resting place of about 3,000 bodies, many of them deceased patients of Austin State Hospital, called the Texas State Lunatic Asylum when patients were first admitted in May 1861.

Even more of the graves represent former residents of the Austin State School and the Travis State School for the mentally retarded. In most cases, the deceased were indigent, and represent only about a third of the patients who died at the hospital.

When the bodies were transferred from the Guadalupe Street location to 51st Street, they were simply buried in a shroud. Each grave was marked with a numbered wooden stick, and those sticks either vanished or disintegrated years ago.

Newer burials were provided with a simple pine box and indicated with a small flat slab bearing the patients identification number. Most of those slabs sank into the ground years ago.

All State Hospital gravestones made after 1998 include the name and dates of birth and death.

One of the more gruesome areas of the cemetery is dedicated to body parts. During the second half of the twentieth century, the hospital conducted autopsies and some surgeries. They buried the body parts in one row of the cemetery.

In addition to the newer cemetery location, many ghost hunters are interested in the site of the old cemetery. Nearby, the Austin State Hospital's administrative building—formerly the lunatic asylum—is the third oldest standing public building in Texas.

More Austin Cemeteries

If you enjoy photographing cemeteries—old and new— or like them for ghost hunting, you may want to visit some of these locations. Others, as noted, are not recommended, but they're included in case someone suggests them in error. This is a partial list, and not all locations have been verified.

Assumption Cemetery, 3650 South I-35, near St. Edward University. Opened in 1953, and privately maintained, this cemetery is too new to be of interest to most ghost hunters.

Barton Springs Baptist Church, 2107 Goodrich Avenue. This small African-American cemetery is in back of the church and next to an apartment complex. Fewer than a dozen headstones remain, and most have been broken or are difficult to read.

Bethany Cemetery, 1300 block of Springdale Road. This small cemetery was started in the mid-nineteenth century.

Bouldin Cemetery was once at or near 14 S. Sixth Street. The Becker Elementary School, 906 West Milton Street, may have been built over it.

Brown Cemetery—There are several cemeteries with this name, some referring to the Brown family, and others indicating African-American cemeteries. Most of them are very small, privately maintained, and on private land.

One "Brown Cemetery" that may interest ghost hunters is part of local folklore. According to legend, Mr. Brown mistreated his slaves badly and was run out of both Louisiana and Mississippi, and moved to Texas. When a slave died, he'd throw the body into a pit on his property, and sow it with limestone to reduce the odor. The pit is supposedly part of Brown Cemetery today, and appropriately haunted, but no one is certain which of the many Brown Cemeteries is the infamous one.

Davis Cemetery, at Vine Street & Cavileer, just south of Northwest District Park, near Shoal Creek. What started in the mid-nineteenth century as a cemetery for the Davis family, grew to include many other families. A wide range of monuments and markers in a quiet residential setting make this an especially attractive cemetery.

Decker Cemetery and Decker Free Church Cemetery are both on Decker Lane near the Methodist Church. Lovely, immaculately kept cemeteries in an area in east Austin that was once a settlement of Swedish immigrants. They're unlikely sites for ghosts, and most of the headstones are too modern—nothing earlier than 1885— to offer historical interest to photographers.

DeMaria Cemetery, 72 Circle S Road. This Hispanic cemetery was established in the late nineteenth century, and remained active through the twentieth century. Located next to an apartment complex, and near the Masonic Cemetery, noted below.

Dessau Lutheran Cemetery, 13300 Dessau Road. Contains a few late nineteenth century stones, but mostly twentieth century markers. One interesting feature of the stones: Most of the early stones are in German script, and very picturesque. (Geb indicates the birth year, and Gest is for the year of death. "Hier Ruhl" means "here lies.")

Fall Creek Cemetery, US Highway 71 West, near South Paleface Ranch Road. This cemetery includes graves from the early nineteenth century through the twentieth century.

Fiskville Cemetery, Fiskville Cemetery Road, off Crown Ridge Road near I-35 and Rundberg Lane. This is a small cemetery with some late nineteenth century headstones, but mostly twentieth century graves.

Fowler Cemetery, also called Grumbles Cemetery and Schneider Cemetery, 52 Brodie Lane, near Home Depot. This is a very small cemetery, and most of the marked headstones represent members of the Grumbles family from the late nineteenth and early twentieth centuries. (Also see Chapter One, including more hauntings at this Home Depot.)

Gregg School Cemetery, 53 Gregg Lane. It's reportedly one of the most beautiful unkempt cemeteries in the Austin area. The few marked graves are on top of a hill, amid weeds and a lovely view. However, it's also on private land.

Hancock Family Cemetery, Steiner Ranch Subdivision, at Burks Lane and Burks Cove. The graves include four marked sites of children from first half of the twentieth century, enclosed by an iron fence.

Jolly Cemetery, 8600 Spicewood Springs Road. As many as half of the graves at this old cemetery may be unmarked. Jolly cemetery was active from around 1870 through 1929, and is now surrounded by apartment complexes. The cemetery's name comes from John Grey Jolly, who was a blacksmith in Jollyville and purchased this land for a cemetery. Some of the old markers and monuments are unusual and very picturesque for photographers. There are no known ghost stories associated with it.

Live Oak Cemetery, Twin Creeks Road, near I-35 and FM 1626 (Onion Creek Road). With more than 1,500 graves on about fifteen well-maintained acres, this cemetery is a favorite among ghost hunters. The oldest headstone seems to be from 1874, but this cemetery has many intriguing features that make it worth a daytime visit. If you'd like to look in at night, the cemetery is surrounded by a chain link fence, and has gravel roads. (Like most Austin cemeteries, Live Oak closes at dusk.)

Longview Cemetery, 7609 Longview Road, south of William Cannon Drive and east of Brodie Lane. This odd little cemetery is in the middle of Longview Park, and close to a basketball court. A tall, locked, chain-link fence protects most of the grave markers. However, there may be many more unmarked graves in back of the fenced-off area.

Look for "grave sinks," which are depressed areas in the topsoil. That's where people were buried in wooden coffins, and the wood rotted over time. The ground over it sank, and it's one way to identify a likely unmarked grave.

Or, some people have success using dowsing rods to locate unmarked graves. In addition, some dowsers can determine far more information about the deceased—and the ghosts—at unmarked graves.

It's never smart to go ghost hunting alone, but in this case, the warnings are doubled. Many ghost hunters have reported strong, malicious energy around this cemetery.

Masonic Cemetery, 76 Circle S Road, just south of William Cannon Drive and I-35. This cemetery is also called the Boggy Creek Cemetery and Old Onion Creek Masonic Cemetery. It contains some very late nineteenth century graves, but mostly mid- to late twentieth century headstones.

Austin Memorial Park Cemetery, 2800 Hancock Drive, is well-known for the clicking and other odd noises that its ghosts make around dusk. By day, it looks like any other well-kept cemetery. However, as sunset approaches, spectral energy surges and even hardy ghost hunters have left the site in a hurry.

**Haunted Austin
Memorial Park
Cemetery.**
Photo by the author.

Mount Calvary Cemetery, I-35 and Manor Street, across from the University of Texas. Some of Austin's earliest settlers are buried in this cemetery that opened around 1870. The cemetery is on the east side of I-35, not far from Oakwood Cemetery. One of the most famous headstones in this cemetery is at its southwest corner, where the marker simply says, "HELLO."

Oak Grove Cemetery, at Spicewood Springs Road and Bull Creek. Small cemetery. Some graves are next to the church, and others are across the road.

Oliver Cemetery, near Oliver Road North and US-290, opened 1858. Fenced and semi-maintained, this cemetery contains nearly 200 graves from the mid-nineteenth century to the present, some of which are unmarked.

Perry Cemetery, 2000 block of Hallshire Court. Mostly late nineteenth century headstones, and some very early twentieth century graves.

Plummers Cemetery, East 12 Street and Springdale Road, adjoining Givens Park. This cemetery is near Oakwood Annex Cemetery, listed above.

Pond Springs Cemetery, Lake Creek Parkway and Rural Route 620, near Wal-Mart and an apartment complex. At the far north edge of Austin in a rapidly growing area, this cemetery is alternately overgrown and well manicured. If you visit it, bring bug spray. The cemetery was active through the late twentieth century. Some of the most intriguing headstones are for nineteenth century "consorts," perhaps the "kept women" of the men who erected their markers. Many ghost hunters praise this cemetery for its eerie atmosphere and powerful spiritual energy.

Tarleton Cemetery at the Barton Creek Mall is behind a locked gate that's on posted, private property. It's a tranquil piece of land just feet from the busy Capital of Texas Highway, with only a few visible graves. Unfortunately, some ghost websites talk about the haunted Tarleton Cemetery when they mean the Tucker Cemetery, described below. The Tarleton Cemetery is not open to the public, and ghost hunters should not try to visit it.

Tucker Cemetery, Stoneridge Road (also called Old Stone Ridge Road), near the Capital of Texas Highway and Rudy's BBQ restaurant. Although the headstones are generally from the early twentieth century to the present day, this cemetery has several ghost stories.

The most popular tale describes a ghost of a young woman who was killed and her body badly mangled when some of her friends hit her while driving with their headlights off. Now, she wanders the woods nearby and protects the many children buried in Tucker Cemetery.

The problem with this story is that Tucker Cemetery— sometimes nicknamed "the baby cemetery" or "the children's cemetery"— is an average, slightly rural cemetery with an average number of children's graves.

Walnut Creek Cemetery, at I-35 on the north side of Braker Lane. At the time of this writing, Walnut Creek Cemetery was overgrown, neglected, and in very bad condition. It's believed to be an African-American cemetery. Only about half of the seventy graves have markers, and most of them are from the first part of the twentieth century.

Williamson Creek Cemetery, 10 Little Texas Lane. This cemetery is just north of William Cannon Drive. The oldest headstone with a date seems to be from 1863. The majority of dated headstones are from the twentieth century, but at least half of the markers have no dates.

Texas Cemetery Laws

Ghost hunters should always check local laws regarding access to cemeteries. In Austin, most public cemeteries are closed between dusk and dawn, and most private cemeteries require specific permission to visit.

These are the relevant Texas state laws:

§ 711.041. Access to Cemetery

(a) Any person who wishes to visit a cemetery or private burial grounds for which no public ingress or egress is available shall have the right to reasonable ingress and egress for the purpose of visiting the cemetery or private burial grounds. This right of access extends only to visitation during reasonable hours and only for purposes usually associated with cemetery visits.

(b) The owner or owners of the lands surrounding the cemetery or private burial grounds may designate the routes of reasonable ingress and egress. Added by Acts 1993, 73rd Leg., ch. 634, § 22, eff. Sept. 1, 1993.

In addition, state laws exist to protect cemeteries from vandalism, theft and desecration. For example, Section 28.03(f) of the Texas Penal Code states that damage to a human burial site—including an offense involving graffiti—is a state jail felony.

Columbus City Cemetery, Columbus, Texas. *Photo by the author.*

CHAPTER FOUR:
MORE EERIE PLACES AROUND AUSTIN

COLUMBUS AND THE TWENTY-YEAR FEUD

Columbus, Texas, is one of the most peaceful—but profoundly haunted—towns in the state, with a lengthy history as the oldest surveyed and platted town in Texas. It's about an hour and a half southeast of Austin.

Columbus is a charming, small town with rolling hills, broad expanses of open land, and fewer than 4,000 residents. Magnificent oak and magnolia trees shelter its lovely, quiet streets, and the downtown looks like a set from the movie, The Music Man.

Don't let appearances fool you. Columbus is so haunted, some say that it's like a ghost hunters' theme park.

Despite its tidy, quiet streets and consistently pleasant residents, Columbus has a violent history, including feuds and shootouts that could rival any "Wild West" movie.

Every episode in Columbus' turbulent history has resulted in ghosts and hauntings.

Columbus appeared on early Spanish maps as a Native American village called Montezuma. The first white settlers arrived around Christmas of 1821, and the town was scheduled to be the headquarters of the Austin colony. However, within a couple of years, Indian attacks and flooding from the Colorado River made Austin choose another location.

Some settlers stayed in Columbus, including Benjamin Beason (or Beeson) who operated a ferry crossing at the Colorado River, and was a leading employer with a gristmill, a sawmill, and a gin. His large home served as an inn, and the Beason family was very successful.

In 1836, during the Texas Revolution, Sam Houston and his men camped near Beason's Crossing. Houston then decided that it would be better to take a stand further east against Santa Anna. As the Republican Army left Columbus, Houston's men burned every building— including Beason's businesses—to the ground.

A year later, Columbus was being rebuilt with a focus on public houses and gambling. By the end of the nineteenth century, Columbus was known for its horses, including a 200-acre racetrack complex and one of Texas' most productive horse-raising enterprises.

In 1839, Robert Robson moved to Columbus from Scotland, and built a three-story castle just north of town. The building had a moat and drawbridge, a large ballroom, a rooftop garden, and it was one of the first Texas buildings with running water.

During the 1850s, Columbus—and surrounding Colorado County—saw a huge increase in plantations. The economy began to lean towards cotton and cattle. Slaves were purchased to work on the ranches, and the county's population was approximately one third African American.

This led to another violent episode in Columbus' history.

Columbus' 1856 Uprising

In Columbus in September 1856, over 200 blacks and—according to the Galveston newspaper—"every Mexican in the county" had organized an uprising. The newspaper claimed that their intent was to murder "the entire white population" with the exception of the young ladies who would be taken captive and made wives of the insurgents.

The well-organized uprising was scheduled for late on the night of September 6th. A series of raids by officials thwarted their plans and over 200 slaves were arrested. The newspaper reported that two were whipped to death and three were hung "in compliance with the unanimous voice of the citizens of the county." Most of the others were "severely punished under the lash."

When the Civil War began, Columbus and Colorado County voted in favor of secession. However, as the war dragged on, it affected both slave labor and the plantation economy. The value of farms dropped to about ten percent of their pre-war worth, and the price of livestock dropped in half, devastating the community.

Columbus was a tinderbox, and Federal troops occupied the city from 1865 through 1870. It didn't help when the Yankee soldiers put newly-free slaves in uniform and empowered them to keep the peace.

Despite this turbulence, Columbus continued to grow. The railroad arrived in Columbus in 1869. As a result of this new, cheaper shipping method, Columbus' cotton economy began to improve. And, within about ten years, cottonseed oil had become an important commodity, and the Columbus Oil Company was created.

Tragedy also struck Texas in this era, when deadly fevers killed thousands. Hundreds of victims of the 1873 yellow fever epidemic were buried in unmarked graves in Columbus' Old City Cemetery and Odd Fellows Rest Cemetery.

Meanwhile, rivalries and conflicts were brewing in Columbus yet again. One of the largest and most infamous was a feud between the Staffords and the Townsends.

The Stafford-Townsend Conflicts

The Townsend family had been in Columbus since the late 1830s, and by the mid-1840s owned over 1,000 acres of land. Asa Townsend (1795 - 1876) was a civic leader and one of Colorado County's leading cattlemen, and a dozen of his children settled in Colorado County.

Robert Earl "Bob" Stafford moved to Colorado County around 1858. After the Civil War, he successfully drove a herd of cattle to Kansas, and that was the beginning of his fortune. He soon moved nearly a dozen of his brothers and sisters to Columbus, and built several businesses.

Robert Stafford, ghost of the Stafford Opera House.

R. E. (Bob) STAFFORD

Colorado County court records document several Columbus rivalries, including an 1872 hearing in which Sumner Townsend was accused of "bearing a deadly weapon." That was followed by a later hearing in which Bob Stafford was accused of "intent to murder" Sumner Townsend.

By 1882, Bob Stafford was one of the richest men in town and formed his own private bank; the vault is still displayed on the first floor of the haunted Stafford Opera House in Columbus.

The economy was shifting in significant ways. Ranches were being fenced with barbed wire. This created a conflict with open-rangers and cattle rustlers, sometimes called "fence cutters."

The Staffords were famous for killing anyone whom they suspected of cattle rustling.

The year 1882 was also the year when James Light Townsend—formerly accused of stealing cattle—was elected Colorado County Sheriff. This escalated the feud between the Townsends, described as "the settled aristocrats" and the Staffords, the "aggressive newcomers."

But, when Bob Stafford wasn't trying to unseat Sheriff Townsend, he was forging ahead with business ventures.

In 1883, Stafford tore down Robson's Castle, which had been damaged by an 1869 flood. Stafford replaced it with his own Columbus Meat and Ice Company.

In 1884, he foreclosed on the Columbus Oil Company.

Stafford built the Stafford Opera House in 1886, which opened with the play, "As in a Looking Glass," featuring Lillian Russell. The building by architect N. J. Clayton remains one of the dominating landmarks in downtown Columbus. During its heyday, special trains brought guests from distant towns for performances in Columbus.

However, downtown Columbus is where the Stafford-Townsend rivalry exploded in 1890, across the street from the Stafford Opera House.

The Colorado County Feud

After the 1890 Fourth of July parade and barbecue, about 3,000 people gathered in downtown Columbus to see the Masons lay the cornerstone for the new Colorado County courthouse. Then, most people returned home or to their lodgings, to prepare for the big dance at the Opera House.

About an hour before the dance, Bob Stafford argued with City Marshal Larkin Hope; Hope was Sheriff James Light Townsend's nephew. The story varies widely—even today, some people choose sides in this dispute—but it concluded when Larkin Hope and his brother, Marion Hope, shot and killed Bob Stafford and his brother, John.

According to most accounts, the dance was still held in the Opera House that night, just feet away from the murders.

Shortly after that, the economy of Columbus faltered badly as Stafford's many businesses—including the meat and ice plant as well as the opera house—closed.

That began an era of violence in Columbus, though the Colorado County feud exploded after a later event involving Larkin Hope.

When Sheriff Townsend died in 1884, his deputy (and cousin by marriage) Sam Reese replaced him. His reelection seem certain until Larkin Hope decided to run against him, and Hope was backed by Marcus "Mark"

Townsend, a state official with a powerful political machine of his own. Until Hope announced himself as a candidate, Townsend had backed Reese. When Townsend shifted his support to Hope, some people in the Reese camp became angry.

Larkin Hope was shot in a downtown Columbus alley shortly before the election. He was brought to the pharmacy at the corner of Spring and Travis Streets where he died. James Coleman, a friend of the Reese family, was indicted for the murder.

Reese was voted out of office and shot dead in another downtown gunfight that also took the life of an innocent bystander. Marion Hope and Mark Townsend were among the men accused of the murders.

Downtown Columbus became known as "Hell's Half Acre," and the town's economy was severely damaged as people avoided the area. It didn't help when the police force was dismissed in an attempt to reduce the city's budget. And, in 1902, when the White Man's Party effectively replaced the Democratic party, racial tension rose dramatically.

By 1906, the city of Columbus was unincorporated. Legally, it no longer existed.

Over twenty years later, law was restored and the town was reincorporated. Tempers cooled somewhat when Sheriff Light Townsend's daughter, Carrie Townsend, married Joe W. Stafford. Bitter memories faded, slowly.

Today, though many people clearly recall the feud and the rivalries, visitors to this peaceful town may have no idea that its past was so violent…unless they are looking for the many ghosts that haunt Columbus.

Where to Ghost Hunt in Columbus

Columbus has enough haunted sites to fill a book. These are some favorites:

When you visit Columbus, you may want to stay at Magnolia Oaks Bed & Breakfast—and The Little Red House—both at 634 Spring Street. It was once the home of Texas state senator Marcus "Mark" Townsend. He backed his cousin, Larkin Hope, for sheriff opposite incumbent Sam Reese, who was a Townsend cousin by marriage. Larkin Hope's assassination marked the beginning of the Colorado County feud. Mark Townsend was among those linked to the later killing of Sam Reese.

Hometown Hall Antiques, at 1120 Milam Street, was once the Red Elk Saloon and Gambling Hall, with a colorful clientele that returns in spirit to recall its bawdy days. In the 1890s, the building was used as a hardware store and undertaking business. The mortuary elevator—used to raise and lower bodies as they were prepared for burial—is in the back of the shop and is very haunted.

In 1890, just outside this building, Bob Stafford and his brother, John—possibly unarmed—were shot by Larkin Hope and his brother, Marion.

When the Texas Paranormal Researchers visited this magnificent antiques shop in July 2006, many members felt the eerie energy around the elevator and some captured orbs in digital photos.

A few minutes after the ghost hunters left the shop, the shop manager heard a chiming sound near the mortuary elevator. When he looked for the source of the sound, he couldn't find anything. Shortly after that, the spirits gave him a rare, antique yardstick; he found it at his feet, also without any explanation.

The Turner-Chapman Gallery at 1038 Milam Street, is less than a block away from Hometown Hall Antiques. This is where Larkin Hope died after he was shot in a nearby alley. The exposed bricks inside the gallery seem to radiate with energy from the past.

Artist Ken Turner is internationally famous for his "ghost paintings," including a painting of the Stafford Opera House that features the image of Bob Stafford's widow as—distraught—she drove her carriage along Spring Street. At the time Mr. Turner painted this, he didn't know about her ghost; he simply felt prompted to include the woman in the picture.

If you'd like to go ghost hunting where Larkin Hope was shot, visit 1014 Milam Street, the home of the Live Oak Art Center. According to some legends, Hope was assassinated in the alley next to it.

The address 1014 Milam Street was also Charles Brunson's saloon—politely called "a dispenser of wines and liquors"—from 1891 until about 1919. Upstairs, an opera house provided entertainment. With its colorful history, there's certain to be some orb energy and possibly some EVP around this building. For the best photos, visit at dusk or immediately after dark.

Mr. Stafford, who was murdered within sight of the building that bears his name, may haunt the opera house. He's seen at the street corner, inside the building, and strolling briskly in front of it, on his way to his home.

His wife may also be one of the ghosts of downtown Columbus. She was visiting just a few blocks away when she heard the shots that killed her husband and his brother. Fearing the worst, she raced down the street too late to prevent the tragedy.

If you see the filmy shape of a woman in a flowing white gown running towards the Opera House, it may be Mrs. Stafford's ghost. This is probably a residual energy imprint that lingers from the tragedy, as the scene repeats regularly and without variation.

The Stafford Opera House is one of Columbus' most magnificent landmarks. It's also nicely haunted by Mr. Stafford and others. Take a tour of the building to see Bob Stafford's bank vault, still in its original location.

Upstairs, ghosts haunt backstage and in several places on the balcony. Check the second through fourth rows in the balcony's center section, and the front of the right side of the balcony as you face the stage.

Outside, you may find a cold spot on the stairs leading to the second floor of the Opera House. It's about one-third of the way up from the street level. And, in the early morning hours, it's haunted by the figure of the "lady in gray," whose spirit tells an odd story.

Haunted staircase at the side of the Stafford Opera House. The Lady in Gray appears here. *Photo by the author.*

Notes from the Other Side

The lady in gray claims that she was a wealthy woman. She'd been engaged to a rogue for about six years. He continually postponed the marriage, and the woman's friends insisted that he was spending time with loose women.

One night, the lady in gray visited the Opera House with two of her friends. Looking down from the balcony, she saw her beloved with his arm around a woman in a low-cut, red dress. As he nuzzled her neck, the lady in gray stared in horror. Then, she composed herself, rose from her seat, and left the theater.

As she tells the story, she had her servants pack the house and sell it, while she left immediately for Atlanta. There, she married a wealthy man, had several children, and lived happily ever after.

However, this is an odd tale. If her life was otherwise happy, why would she haunt the Opera House?

She may have been a member of the Stafford family. They were wealthy and had ties to Georgia.

During early morning hours, I've captured some vivid pictures showing an orb at the exact spot where others have felt a "cold spot" on the stairs.

I recommend taking ghost photos at dusk or after dark, from the sidewalk at the foot of the stairs.

The former fiancé…? He'd been living on credit, anticipating a handsome allowance from his marriage to the woman in gray. He was forced to leave town in haste, and spent the rest of his life as a professional gambler. He never married.

If you wait at the stairs after the woman in gray vanishes, you may see the frantic fiancé appear briefly at the top of the stairs. Then he turns and disappears as he goes back through the door to the Opera House.

In the July 2006 investigation, one member of Texas Paranormal Researchers took a very clear daytime photo showing the lady in gray reflected in an Opera House window. It's wise to take a lot of photos around the Opera House; study them carefully for hidden anomalies and evidence of ghosts.

Columbus City Cemetery

Columbus City Cemetery—also called the "Old City Cemetery"—at 1300 Walnut Street is one of two profoundly haunted cemeteries in Columbus. The vast majority of graves are unmarked and many represent victims of the 1873 yellow fever epidemic. They surround the headstones and monuments in the center of this enormous, fenced field.

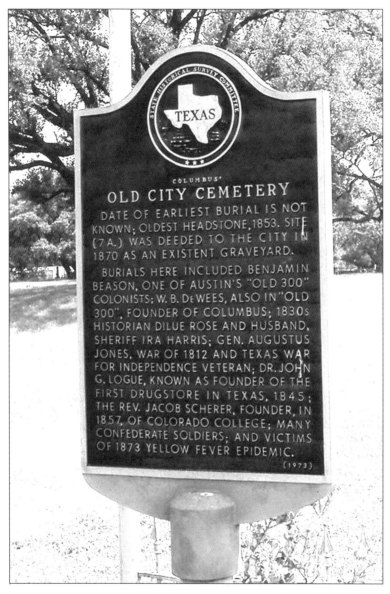

STATE HISTORICAL SURVEY COMMITTEE

TEXAS

COLUMBUS'
OLD CITY CEMETERY
DATE OF EARLIEST BURIAL IS NOT
KNOWN; OLDEST HEADSTONE, 1853. SITE
(7A.) WAS DEEDED TO THE CITY IN
1870 AS AN EXISTENT GRAVEYARD.

BURIALS HERE INCLUDED BENJAMIN
BEASON, ONE OF AUSTIN'S "OLD 300"
COLONISTS; W. B. DeWEES, ALSO IN "OLD
300", FOUNDER OF COLUMBUS; 1830s
HISTORIAN DILUE ROSE AND HUSBAND,
SHERIFF IRA HARRIS; GEN. AUGUSTUS
JONES, WAR OF 1812 AND TEXAS WAR
FOR INDEPENDENCE VETERAN; DR. JOHN
G. LOGUE, KNOWN AS FOUNDER OF THE
FIRST DRUGSTORE IN TEXAS, 1845;
THE REV. JACOB SCHERER, FOUNDER, IN
1857, OF COLORADO COLLEGE; MANY
CONFEDERATE SOLDIERS; AND VICTIMS
OF 1873 YELLOW FEVER EPIDEMIC.

(1973)

Historic marker, Columbus City Cemetery. *Photo by the author.*

The monuments at the center of the field are among the most beautiful in Texas, making this one of the state's most photogenic cemeteries.

The kneeling angel monument marks one of this cemetery's most haunted graves. In the early morning hours as the sun is coming up, you may see some very clear orbs in your flash photos around the angel figure.

Haunted angel monument, Columbus City Cemetery.
Photo by the author.

That is the grave of Phillip Kretschmer of Maffersdorf, Bohemia, whose 1897 obituary described him as an "old-time" businessman although he died at age forty-eight "after a three weeks' illness of inflammation of the bowels and other maladies."

The newspaper also said, "Mr. Kretschmer was of a quiet, unobtrusive disposition, attending strictly to his own business, and had many friends among those who knew him best." A reference was made to bereaved relatives, but no immediate family was mentioned.

Further study of Mr. Kretschmer's life and early death may provide clues to this haunting. Or, his spirit may be trying to communicate to us.

A victim of King Tut's Curse is also buried in Columbus City Cemetery. His name was Jonathan W. Sargent and he was killed in a car accident in 1928, six years after he assisted Howard Carter at Tutankhamen's tomb.

Another grave is the resting place of a man jokingly called "King Tut." His body was repeatedly re-embalmed so that people with missing relatives could view it. After several years when no one identified it, the figure was so rigid from embalming fluid, he was mummified; he was eventually buried, identity unknown.

Columbus City Cemetery monument. *Photo by the author.*

Even More Haunted Places in Columbus

Columbus Odd Fellows Rest Cemetery at 1500 Montezuma Street features the graves of Robert "Bob" Stafford and his brother John, as well as the man who was involved in their deaths, Larkin Hope.

Like Columbus City Cemetery, the graves—marked and unmarked—include the remains of victims of yellow fever.

The Odd Fellows Cemetery was very different when it was deeded in 1871. The bluff on the south side of the cemetery soon eroded, exposing some graves. In 1888, a committee formed to prevent further damage, but they could not save the grave of Henry Middleton, which washed out completely. In 1901, additional land was added to deter erosion.

After a flood in 1913, some gravestones were moved for safety from the City Cemetery to the Odd Fellows Cemetery.

This is just the tip of the iceberg in Columbus. With the number of 19th-century gambling houses, saloons, and shootouts, you could probably find orbs and EVP almost anywhere in downtown Columbus.

Beason's Park, just outside of town on Highway 90, is near the early site of Benjamin Beason's home, inn, ferry, and other businesses. It's a beautiful setting and also worth investigating for orbs and especially EVP.

Researchers also report excellent results with dowsing rods at haunted Columbus sites, so it's worth exploring with divinatory tools as well.

Columbus is a wonderful town to visit, and its history makes it a must-see for serious ghost hunters in the Austin area.

Each year in early November, Columbus celebrates history with their Live Oaks & Dead Folks Cemetery Tour. This popular event is staged at a local cemetery, and includes graveside performances by re-enactors representing nineteenth and early twentieth century ghosts. For authenticity, a local historian writes the scripts. Advance tickets are recommended. For more information contact the Nesbitt Memorial Library at 979-732-5514.

While you are in a Columbus, be sure to stop at Jerry Mikeska's BBQ restaurant, at exit 698 from I-10. in addition to delicious and affordable food, you'll have an extraordinary view of over 150 hunting trophies and stuffed animals... real ones. Some people are troubled by the beady stares of all those glass eyes, but many ghost hunters considered it an appropriate place to dine before or after a visit to haunted sites.

Columbus is located at the intersection of Interstate 10 and Texas State Highway 71.

EVEN MORE TRULY TERRIFYING HAUNTS NEAR AUSTIN

Many places near Austin offer great ghost hunting opportunities. Some are popular tourist destinations, and others are genuine ghost towns. Since the most eerie ghost activity takes place after dark, you'll probably want to spend the night at some of these alarmingly haunted spots.

The Devil's Backbone

One of the most famous and most beautiful haunted areas in Texas is called the Devil 's Backbone. The region includes nine canyons covering more than 4,500 acres, and gets its name from a narrow ridge of large hills over 1,000 feet in elevation.

In the middle of the nineteenth century, Comanches and Kiowas hid among these hills to observe the arrival and activities of settlers. However, the ghostly history of the Devil's Backbone began centuries earlier.

The range of spirits at the Devil's Backbone is as extraordinary and varied as the history of this region. Sightings include groups of Native Americans to a miner and his family, and even a company of Confederate soldiers on horseback.

Battles are reenacted, an American Indian nicknamed "Draco" herds his ghostly cattle through the hills, and the ghost of a Spanish monk appears to glow as he walks solemnly through the valleys.

Most visitors to The Devil's Backbone feel as if someone unseen is watching them. Others smell smoke from a campfire, in an area where no campfires are allowed. Many hear footsteps nearby, but never see anyone who'd cause them.

Some of the more unusual ghosts include an apparition, which has appeared at the front of cars driving along Purgatory Road near Wimberley, Texas.

Jacob's Well in Wimberley is known as one of the most dangerous places to go diving. At least eight experienced divers have lost their lives in its caverns. After dark, "ghost lights" have been spotted near the well.

In rare cases, people have felt possessed by a spirit—sometimes a wolf—who speaks through them and describes the tragic loss of Native lives, lands, and their way of life. This spirit never harms its hosts, but can talk for several hours before leaving.

Because so much paranormal activity takes place after dark at the Devil's Backbone, you'll want to spend the night there.

Visitors often stay at the Stage Stop Ranch near Wimberley, at the southern end of the Devil's Backbone. It has its own haunted history as a stagecoach stop since the 1860s. It's perfect for taking photos from the comfort of the wrap-around porch of the main house. The rural location almost guarantees that you'll have no interference from city lights.

You'll get a good night's sleep whether you stay in the main house or one of the ranch's nine well-appointed guest cabins. However, if you're up between midnight and two a.m., be sure to take a few photos at the big oak tree at the corner of the main building. The tale of a hanging is probably fiction, but the orbs and possible ectoplasm (unexplained mists) in your photos will be proof of something ghostly at the tree.

EVP may also confirm the residual noises from the many coaches and wagons that pulled into this comfortable ranch during the nineteenth and twentieth centuries.

Notes from the Other Side

According to the spirits, the ghost at the oak tree is a woman who was supposed to meet her fiancé there, shortly after midnight. She thought that they were going to elope, but the young man never showed up. The woman remained at the ranch for a couple of weeks, spending her life's savings. She never gave up hope. When her money was nearly gone, she took a job at the inn, and then found work in a nearby town. From time to time, she'd visit the ranch and ask if her young man had shown up.

She continues to visit the tree with her traveling satchel in hand, hoping that her long-lost love will show up and they'll finally live happily ever after.

Both the Devil's Backbone and the Stage Stop Ranch have been featured on TV shows, including "Unsolved Mysteries" and the Discovery Channel.

Day or night, the Devil's Backbone is a worthwhile drive. Be sure to take your camera, because you'll see some of the most spectacular landscapes in Texas.

The Devil's Backbone extends from southeast of Austin to the town of Wimberley, Texas.

Burnet, Texas

Burnet is northwest of Austin, and has been declared the Bluebonnet Capital of Texas for its profuse display of wildflowers each spring. However, ghost hunters will want photos of more than just the flowers.

Burnet's Texas Star Grill is known for great food, relaxed dining, and the ghost of a previous owner.

From Burnet, take Texas State Highway 29 west to Farm Road 2341 and drive northwest to Spider Mountain, which offers spectacular views overlooking Lake Buchanan.

This spot can also provide great ghost photos. According to legend, this was a large Indian burial site. Ghost hunters report sightings of floating lights and the spirits of the Native Americans who once lived in this area.

And, while you're near Burnet, stop in nearby Joppa. Both of the town's old iron bridges are ideal for EVP recordings. Locals joke that a troll lives there, because they can hear running and heavy breathing from beneath the bridges. If you capture those eerie sounds in a recording, that could be your best memento from your Texas ghost hunts.

Gonzales

Gonzales has been a colorful town from its very beginning. The year it was settled, Indians burned it. Eleven years later, Sam Houston burned the town as he retreated from Mexican forces.

Gonzales was also the only Texas town to send reinforcements to the Battle of the Alamo.

But, before the Alamo, Gonzales was already known for its courageous citizens.

"Come and take it" was the slogan of the first skirmish of the Texas Revolution. In October 1835, when Mexico demanded the return of a bronze cannon used for the defense of Gonzales against Indian attack, the colonists stood firm. When Mexican soldiers arrived in Gonzales to take the cannon by force, the colonists said, "There it is—come and take it."

Lives were lost in the battle that ensued. Almeron Dickinson—whose wife Susanna now haunts her Austin home (see Chapter Two)—was one of the colonists who survived. Along with his partner, Richard Kimble, he had a successful business, the Dickinson and Kimble Hat Factory. Both of these men were among the colonists who claimed victory at Gonzales, and later died at the Alamo.

Ghost hunters should visit the Old Jail Museum at 414 St. Lawrence Street in Gonzales for some great orb photos. The Memorial Museum, which remembers the "Come and take it" battle, is not as reliable for ghostly images, but it's a worthwhile stop for history buffs.

The best ghost encounters are likely to occur at Gonzales Pioneer Village, one-half mile northwest of town on US 183. Every October, the battle is re-enacted, and you're likely to see orbs and pick up EVP at dusk and later in the evening.

But, at any hour of day or night, you can witness a ghost story: The cursed clock of Gonzales.

Gonzales' lovely courthouse is one of eighteen Texas courthouses designed and built by architect James Riely Gordon. Mr. Gordon was famous for his precise designs, and he may be most famous for designing the Arizona Capitol building.

In 1896, as Mr. Riely was completing the Gonzales courthouse, he crowned it with a clock. In fact, the tower has four clocks, each facing in a different direction, so that the citizens could always see the correct time. And, the clocks were perfectly synchronized.

In 1921, as convicted murderer Albert Howard was awaiting death, he studied the clock closely, counting his remaining hours and minutes. The clock became a symbol of what had happened to him. Up to the moment of his death, Howard swore that he was an innocent man.

Watching the clock, Howard got an idea. He announced that, if he was put to death, the clock tower would prove his innocence. He cursed it, saying that the four clock faces— always perfectly synchronized—would never tell the right time again.

On March 21st, 1921, Albert Howard was hung for his crimes. And, from that moment on, the clocks stopped working correctly.

Repairman after repairman was called in, and no one could find anything wrong with it. They cleaned the machinery, oiled it, and…the clocks were still out of sync.

In 1990, the clock was finally repaired…or so some claim. Others report that the clock seems to speed up and then slow down at odd times of day and night. Perhaps Mr. Howard is still angry after all these years.

Before visiting Gonzales, be sure to set your watch to the correct time so that you can check the clocks—all four of them—and see if you can witness Albert Howard's curse.

Gonzales is about an hour and a half south of Austin on US Highway 183.

La Grange's Colorful Past

La Grange, Texas, may be most famous for the Chicken Ranch, the basis for the musical and movie, "The Best Little Whorehouse in Texas." But, that's not La Grange's only claim to fame, especially among ghost hunters.

La Grange began as a stopping point along an old buffalo trail where it crossed the Colorado River. As the trail grew in popularity early in the nineteenth century, so did the town.

One must-see location is the Old City Cemetery on North Jackson at Highway 71 E. It includes graves representing approximately twenty percent of the population of 1867 La Grange, when hundreds died during a yellow fever epidemic.

Sites like this are reliable if you use dowsing rods, record EVP, or measure EMF, as well as for orb photography.

Monument Hill State Historic Site at 414 State Loop 92, one mile south of La Grange, is a tribute to the executed prisoners from the infamous "Black bean" episode, and thirty-six of the victims of the Dawson Massacre. At this location, you can also visit the Kreische Brewery, which maintains the Historic Site. Arrive before the gates close at five p.m.

When you're in La Grange, be sure to stop at the Chamber of Commerce at 171 South Main Street. This used to be the Fayette County Jail, which was built in 1883. It's haunted by Marie Dach, who moves objects—sometimes heavy ones thrown with force—around the former jail.

Marie Dach and her husband, Anton, were immigrants from Germany. However, Anton Dach died of cancer in 1930, leaving Marie with three small children and a farm to run. So, she hired Henry Stoever of Schulenberg to help her.

In February 1933, Henry's brother, Richard, asked the La Grange sheriff to locate Henry. Henry's daughter had received an odd letter from her father, and was concerned.

Deputy Sheriff Jim Flournoy—later connected with the "best little whorehouse" story—investigated at Mrs. Dach's farm, and noticed something odd about her new hen house. Inside, a three-foot by six-foot area looked freshly dug. Just a few feet down, Flournoy found what was left of Henry Stoever. He'd been shot and then his body had been burned.

Mrs. Dach admitted to killing Mr. Stoever, but said that she had been driven to it after "a series of cruelties and indignities" that had followed a "criminal assault" upon her person two months earlier.

On the 25th of May, Marie Dach was convicted of murder and sentenced to die in the electric chair. She was only the second woman to receive the death penalty.

The widow's attorney began filing appeals immediately. But, as Mrs. Dach waited for a new trial, she became depressed and then morose. She refused food, and in late August, she starved herself to death.

Today, the Widow Dach haunts her former cell, which has been ironically converted into the Chambers' refrigerator room.

Notes from the Other Side

Mrs. Dach believed that the killing was a triumph in a situation where she might just as likely have been the victim. She was astonished when the jury—and public sentiment—turned against her. But, she had always been a very logical person...until her involvement with Mr. Stoever, that is.

In her jail cell, Mrs. Dach considered her past and the possible outcome of her appeal. She didn't want to die, but the prospect of spending the rest of her life in confinement wasn't much better.

Mrs. Dach decided to try starving herself, first for attention to what she thought was an unfair verdict. Then, she felt that it might be a reasonable conclusion to her life. After all, she could just as easily been killed by Mr. Stoever and be dead now. Without her children, life was barely worth living anyway.

(It's interesting that she still insists upon calling him Mr. Stoever, and not just "Henry" or "Stoever.")

Mrs. Dach had been saving money to move to another state, near some cousins who'd immigrated to the States. She hid the money and didn't put it in the bank. Then, one day late in 1933, when Stoever threatened further "indignities," Mrs. Dach killed him.

She hoped to save enough money to flee with her children before the body was found.

Mrs. Dach would like her descendants to have that money, but the landmarks have changed too much since she buried it. She can't remember where the money is. But, she is as persistent after death as she was methodical during her lifetime. She's likely to continue haunting regularly, retracing her movements during her last days, until she finds the missing money.

Jefferson, Texas

Jefferson, Texas is a considerable drive from Austin, but—if you're a ghost enthusiast—it's well worth the trip. It's known as one of Texas' most haunted towns.

Jefferson—named after the former American President—has always been the kind of town where every day is a celebration, and no one wants to leave...not even their ghosts. Today, Jefferson looks like a peaceful picture postcard. However, in the nineteenth century, it was a "Wild West" party town with brothels and bars that never closed. Jefferson is where the first beer was brewed in Texas.

Spend a night or two in one of Jefferson's many haunted hotels and B&Bs: Claiborne House, the Excelsior Hotel (ask for the Jay Gould room), the Jefferson Hotel, McKay House, and White Manor Oak all have haunted reputations.

The Jefferson Hotel is my first choice for a comfortable bed and some great ghost hunting. The building started as a cotton warehouse. Upstairs, it was a bordello during Jefferson's wilder days. Later, the structure became a fashionable hotel.

Room 14 is a favorite, thanks to the ghost of the "whispering woman." Room 19 is also popular among ghost hunters. However, every room at the Jefferson Hotel has a colorful history. Take plenty of photos, especially in your room, in the upstairs hallway, and around the stairs. You are likely to find orbs or even a phantom figure among your pictures.

Notes from the Other Side

The Jefferson Hotel is haunted by many happy ghosts. However, one of them is not quite as happy as the others, and he came through during a spiritual reading.

This young man had it all. He was bright, funny, charming, and wealthy. He used to visit the bordello where the Jefferson Hotel is now, and he liked to think that he enjoyed the company of each of the girls, equally.

However, one night after a drunken game of cards with some friends, he made a shocking discovery: He was in love with one of the women of the bordello.

Hoping that it was just a temporary attraction, he left for several months in Europe. However, the bright lights and sophisticated amusements of London and Paris could not diminish the intensity of his emotions.

In time, he returned to the bordello, but the young woman had moved away. Some of the girls said that she'd fallen in love with a fine man, and married him. Others said that she'd tired of the work and moved to another city to start fresh.

The ghost of the wealthy young man lingers at the Jefferson Hotel, sometimes pacing the floor of the room he used to share with his lady love. He's still not sure if he should have proposed marriage to her, but he can't forget her memory.

Jefferson's nightly ghost tours are both fascinating and fun, and open to visitors over age twelve. Call 1-800-299-1593 for reservations; be sure to wear comfortable shoes and bring your camera. You'll visit a wide variety of haunted sites, and hear great stories.

To drive to Jefferson from Austin, take I-35 north and then I-35E to Dallas. Turn east on I-20 and exit at Route 59 North. The trip will take you about six hours, so plan to spend at least one night in Jefferson. Most ghost investigations are so successful, researchers stay two nights in this very haunted town.

Lockhart, Texas

Lockhart is 30 miles south of Austin, and—in the 1870s—it was the southernmost point of the Chisholm Trail. Today, it's best known as the "Barbecue Capital of Texas."

In 1840, this town was called Plum Creek, and it was the site of a terrible battle involving settlers and Indians.

It was a sultry August day when more than 600 Comanches sacked the nearby town of Linnville, Texas. The Comanches had been terrorizing the area for a considerable period of time. Both the settlers and the other Native American nations were tired of the fighting.

It was August 11th when a large group of settlers and the Tonkawa Indians waited for the Comanches at Plum Creek. The latter tribe was traveling slowly due to the large amount of loot that they were hauling back to their homes.

What followed was an extraordinary scene of death and destruction that has led to equally dramatic hauntings.

The Battle of Plum Creek was swift and vicious. At least eighty Comanches died, but only one Texan lost his life in the fight. Afterwards—at least according to some legends—the Tonkawa roasted and ate pieces of the dead Comanches. The Comanches never attacked a town again, and retreated from central Texas altogether.

This battle is re-enacted every May as part of the Chisholm Trail Roundup. Like many re-enactments, ghosts often appear among those who are participating in the performance. Late at night, other ghosts have been spotted, continuing to battle their enemies.

While you're in Lockhart, stop at the Caldwell County Museum. It used to be the county courthouse, with the county jail occupying the top floors. Today, ghost hunters report strong residual energy hauntings throughout the building. When this book was written, the museum was open only on weekend afternoons.

Marble Falls

If you're an experienced EVP (Electronic Voice Phenomena) enthusiast, take your digital voice recorder to Marble Falls' famous Dead Man's Hole, off County Road 401. It's a natural 155-foot deep hole. In the nineteenth century, a tree limb used to extend over the hole. The tree was used for lynchings, and—when the victim was dead—

the hangman would cut the rope so that the body fell into the hole.

Today, the hole is covered with a protective grate and a historical marker provides more of the story.

Ghost hunters report successful EVP recordings even during daytime hours. The voices seem to be coming from deep inside the hole, which was a grave for many unfortunate men.

Notes from the Other Side

There are several ghosts at this site, and all of them have a story to tell. Unfortunately, it's the same story each time. The spirits claim that they were unjustly accused of crimes that they never committed. They claim that at least one man—probably the hangman—was the actual criminal. They'd like the to set the record straight.

In addition, that guilty man may haunt the area around Dead Man's Hole.

This isn't a "fun" haunting, and it's not a recommended destination after mid-afternoon. Never go there alone. This is strictly a stop for experienced ghost hunters with nerves of steel.

Round Rock, Texas

The city of Round Rock is north of Austin and the scene of a famous shootout that is re-enacted every July during the town's Frontier Days.

Sam Bass was a local character best known for racing horses, robbing stagecoaches and holding up banks.

Original *wanted* poster for Sam Bass.

On July 19th, in 1878, Bass and his two-man gang were on their way to rob a bank. Deputy Sheriff A. W. Grimes saw Bass and asked if he was carrying a gun. Bass replied by drawing his pistol and shooting Grimes dead.

During the gunfire, Bass' companion, Seaborn Barnes, was shot in the head and the other gang member, Frank Jackson, got away.

Bass also suffered wounds and died on his birthday two days later. He was buried at the old Round Rock Cemetery on a street that is known today as Sam Bass Road, near the old slave cemetery.

Bass's ghost has been seen at the site of the shootout, and sometimes at his grave. A remorseful Frank Jackson sometimes appears at the gravesite and tips his hat in respect before walking off and then vanishing in thin air.

Notes from the Other Side

Sam Bass was a happy-go-lucky young man plagued by an unhappy romance and a sense that his successes were never enough. He still suspects that someone betrayed him. He is reasonably certain that Deputy Sheriff Grimes didn't "just happen to be there" when the trio were on their way to the bank. Bass isn't certain who shot him in the back, but his spirit revisits Round Rock regularly, hoping for a face-to-face confrontation with the man who caused his death.

While you're in Round Rock, be sure to go on the Round Rock Ghost Tours. Owners Leigh and Dayne Choate will show you where to encounter the ghosts of Sam Bass, A. W. Grimes, and other colorful characters from Round Rock's Wild West past.

And, if you dine at Saradora's, a popular hometown coffeehouse with live music at night, ask the staff about being "grimed" by the ghost of the deputy sheriff.

HAUNTED FORTS AND REAL GHOST TOWNS NEAR AUSTIN

In Texas, forts were established to protect settlers and travelers from Indian attacks.

Between Native attacks, slave uprisings, the Texas Revolution, and the lawlessness of the early "Wild West," dozens of forts were established in Texas from the 1680s through more modern times.

Almost every fort has a ghost story or two. Some are folklore while others have been witnessed by thousands of visitors, and are strongly rooted in history. This is an overview of a few haunted forts near Austin, Texas.

Ghosts In and Around the Alamo

The Alamo is not only Texas' most famous fort, but also one of its most haunted. Located at the heart of San Antonio—about an hour and a half from Austin—the site is a must-see for tourists and ghost hunters alike.

The Alamo, West Elevation. *Photo by Arthur W. Stewart for Historic American Buildings Survey, 8 Apr 1936.*

Ghosts were first sighted at the Alamo in late in 1836, after the fall of the Alamo.

Under orders from General Antonio López de Santa Anna, Colonel Andrade directed his soldiers to demolish the remains of the Alamo and its chapel, the Mission San Antonio de Valero, which had been established in 1718.

However, as the soldiers approached the remains of the Alamo, six ghostly figures emerged from the chapel walls, waving flaming swords above their heads and ordering the soldiers not to touch the Alamo.

The soldiers fled and reported what had happened to their commander.

Andrade responded by calling for his horse and a cannon. Leading his men back to the Alamo, he intended to prove what cowards they were.

Instead, the ghostly figures reappeared, forcing Andrade and his men to retreat. However, as Andrade glanced back at the Alamo, he saw fire break out in several locations. According to one legend, the smoke from the fires formed a large, threatening figure that tossed balls of fire as Andrade's terrified men as they ran away in fear.

Others claim that they saw the same six figures—described as "diablos" or devils—marching towards them carrying balls of fire.

Some people speculate that the ghosts were angry monks who'd established the mission and served both Indians and settlers for nearly 100 years before the Spanish claimed ownership of the Alamo.

Or, they may be six Texans who tried to surrender at the conclusion of the battle at the Alamo. They were offered protection by one of Santa Anna's commanders, General Manuel Fernandez de Castrillon. However, Santa Anna refused Castrillon's request, and the six were hacked to death by Santa Anna's soldiers.

Castrillon tried to intervene and was injured during the vicious attack. His ghost also haunts the Alamo.

Others believe that Andrade and his soldiers witnessed the collective energy of the approximately 150 Texas heroes who died defending the Alamo. Their spirits may not rest since they were denied proper burials.

After the Alamo fell to the Spanish on March 6, 1836, Santa Anna ordered the burial of his army's dead at the Campo Santo cemetery. Today, that's at Milam Square and Santa Rosa Hospital.

However, Santa Anna refused to give the Texans proper burials. Instead, he set up pyres around the Alamo and burned the bodies.

A year later, when the new Republic of Texas reclaimed the Alamo, Texan soldiers gathered as many ashes as they could find around the Alamo. According to legend, these were placed in a small coffin and buried in a solemn funeral ceremony.

The exact burial spot is unknown, and the legend may not be true. It's unlikely that, a year later, many of the original ashes were left. In fact, if they could be gathered into "a small coffin," the ashes probably represented a very small percentage of the remains of the Texas heroes.

This may account for some of the many dramatic hauntings at the Alamo, even in broad daylight.

By the late nineteenth century, the Alamo was used by the City of San Antonio as a police station and jail. Almost immediately, prisoners in the old Alamo barracks began to complain about ghostly shadows and moaning. Apparitions patrolled the top of the police station. People heard screams and gunfire, and they smelled smoke.

The jail was soon closed and the prisoners moved to another site.

The Alamo, Arcade Courtyard. *Photo by Arthur W. Stewart for Historic American Buildings Survey, 8 Apr 1936.*

In her book, Texas Haunted Forts, author Elaine Coleman describes ghostly smoke and fire seen around the old Alamo chapel.

She also talks about the ghost of a little blond-haired boy who appears at an upper window of the chapel. Many see him around the anniversary of the Alamo, and especially in early February. He's believed to be a child who survived, but returns to look for his father who was killed in the battle.

He's one of many ghostly children seen around the Alamo, usually during the daytime.

The ghost of another little boy, a Mexican lad, appears at the door of the Alamo. Children and young teens see him, and don't realize that he's a ghost.

Two more children follow tour groups around, and vanish when no one is looking. They're probably the sons of Englishman Anthony Wolfe, who served in Captain William R. Carey's artillery company at the Alamo.

The two boys, ages eleven and twelve, hid in the chapel at the Alamo but were killed by Mexican soldiers anyway. Alamo survivor Susannah Dickinson recalled seeing their lifeless bodies carried out on bayonets.

Another Alamo ghost appears as a dark figure in a long, dark, duster-type coat. Sometimes he strolls around the old fort. At other times, he's spotted on the road from Nacogodoches to San Antonio.

Many people believe that he's Louis Moses Rose, who fought for ten days at the Alamo. Three days before the Alamo fell, he decided that he "wasn't ready to die." The fifty-one-year-old veteran climbed out a window and walked past enemy lines under the cover of darkness.

Others wonder if the apparition is one of the twenty-two riders who rode for William Travis, and vainly tried to summon help for the men who were facing death at the Alamo.

According to legend, he regrets leaving his comrades and is trying to finish the battle with them.

Davy Crockett is among the ghosts of the Alamo. He's wearing his famous buckskins and carrying a rifle.

At sunrise, some people report a tall, thin apparition on top of a roof at the Alamo chapel. He holds a small child in his arms. Colonel Andrade had reported a man and a child who leaped from that roof during the battle.

After dark, a ghostly woman has been spotted next to the well. She looks like a costumed historian, except that she appears only from the waist up.

A more modern ghost also haunts the Alamo: actor John Wayne. According to reports, he became fascinated with Alamo history and lore when he was filming the 1960 movie about the battle. "The Duke" appears to be chatting with some other ghosts around the grounds.

The Alamo is a registered historical landmark and its church is designated as a Texas shrine. Out of respect, no photography is permitted inside the Alamo.

Likewise, EMF detectors and recording devices are not permitted.

However, there are a few Alamo-related sites in other parts of San Antonio.

For example, orbs and ghostly activity has been reported near where Santa Anna built pyres to burn the Texans' bodies. One location is near the San Antonio Marriott River Center, at the corner of Bowie Street and Commerce.

Market Square, about ten blocks from the Alamo, is another haunted location. According to legend, a nearby children's park is the site where Santa Anna buried many of his army's dead. The park is reportedly very haunted.

Of course, the Alamo isn't the only haunted fort in Texas.

More Haunted Forts Near Austin

In Texas' history, some forts like the Alamo were large enough to house dozens of soldiers. Other forts were simply fortified homes, also called camps and sometimes cabins. Many of them remain across the Texas countryside, but even more have vanished. Only historic markers and ghosts linger at the sites.

These are a few of the most haunted sites forts, camps, and cabins in the vicinity of Austin.

Coleman's Fort (also known as Fort Colorado)

The site of the early Fort Colorado is haunted by at least two ghosts: a Comanche shaman and the man who built the fort.

Colonel Robert M. Coleman built Fort Colorado in 1836 saying, "I have selected the most beautiful site I ever saw for the purpose. It is immediately under the foot of the mountains. The eminence is never the less commanding, and in every way suited to the object in view."

After the fort was completed, a Comanche medicine man visited its commander each evening, hoping to find a peaceful solution to the constant battles between the Comanches and the settlers.

Usually, the Indian waited for the nightly fog to rise from the banks of nearby Walnut Creek. Concealed by the mist, he could enter the fort without raising alarm.

Likewise, Colonel Coleman did not mention these visits to his men or to his superiors.

After these clandestine meetings had gone on for several months, the soldiers became suspicious of their commander's behavior. More and more, he kept to his room in the blockhouse at night, and even had his meals sent there.

Worried that their commander was mentally unhinged, the soldiers contacted Coleman's superiors and an investigation was announced.

At first, Coleman was supposed to turn over his command to Major William H. Smith, but refused without further explanation.

In January 1837, superiors in Washington sent another replacement, Captain Micah Andrews.

At this point, Coleman was ready to reveal the secret negotiations that had taken place in the blockhouse. The evening that Andrews arrived, the Comanche shaman walked down the blockhouse stairs to meet Andrews.

However, a soldier saw the Indian and misunderstood what was going on. The soldier raised his rifle and, with one shot, killed the medicine man. Months of delicate negotiations were completely undone.

Colonel Coleman, distraught and disillusioned by military policy, wrote a pamphlet criticizing Sam Houston. For this, he was dismissed from service, and drowned the following July while bathing in the Brazos River. The location of his grave is unknown.

He left a widow and six children. Ironically, Comanches killed his wife and oldest son early in 1839.

Early in 1838, Fort Colorado was abandoned, and its location is indicated by a granite and bronze historical marker.

On foggy nights, the figures of the Comanche medicine man and Colonel Coleman have been seen regularly. It's as if they're still meeting, and trying to find a different solution to the bloody events that followed their failed attempts at peace.

Unexplained lights also appear in the mist, and it is a site where orbs are routine.

The fort was located about two and one half miles northeast of Montopolis Bridge in Austin, at the intersection of FM 969 and Webberville Road. The fort covered a large plot of land, with two two-story blockhouses and several cabins within its stockade walls.

Unearthly Laughter at Woods' Fort

Southeast of Austin at the intersection of State Highway 71 and County Road 117, not far from West Point, a marker stands at the site of Woods' Fort. This fortified homestead was also called Woods' Prairie, named after pioneer Zadock

Woods, who settled at this location with his family. Settlers who were under attack from Indians, often Kiowas or Comanches, found refuge at this site

Reports include whoops from the ghosts of attacking Indians, and unearthly laughter that seems to come from all sides of the surrounding prairie, even in broad daylight.

Bastrop's Haunted Fort Wilbarger

In 1836, a dozen locals were dismembered and scalped by Indians. This was also the site of an earlier attack in 1829, at the Thompson farm.

Castleman's Cabin Massacre

Belmont is a small town about fifteen miles west of Gonzales, and the site of a violent attack.

On April 15, 1835, a bloody massacre took place just outside John Castleman's cabin near Belmont. His home was located at Sandies Creek—formerly called Castleman Creek—along the San Antonio road, a popular route for traders.

The night of April 14th, about a dozen French and Mexican traders stopped at the Castlemans' farm. They declined the Casteman family's offer to stay in the cabin, but preferred to sleep outdoors in a wooded grove not far from the creek.

John Castleman warned the traders that a Comanche war party had been spotted nearby. He explained that his cabin would be safer, but his offer was declined again.

At dawn on the 15th, between sixty and eighty Comanches seemed to appear out of nowhere. They fired rifles and whooped as they rode in, waking the traders who formed barricades with their carts and saddles. For four hours, the Indians and traders shot at each other.

Finally, the Indians reorganized and rushed the traders from three sides, forcing them to fire almost simultaneously. This meant that the traders had to pause and reload at the same time as well. During the silence, the Indians rushed the traders and attacked them hand-to-hand. Outnumbered about six to one, the traders soon lost their fight.

John Castleman and his family witnessed the massacre from their cabin. They dared not to make a sound, and couldn't help the traders or they'd be killed, too. The Indians outnumbered them by a wide margin.

Once the traders were dead, scalped, and stripped of their belongings, the Indians rode off with the traders' mules and horses.

This site is not far from the October 1835 "Come and Take It" battle at Sandies Creek, where Gonzales' men refused to return a cannon to the Mexican military. That event was the beginning of the Texas Revolution.

High EMF at Sandies Creek

Sandies Creek's banks seem to contain a large amount of residual energy that can be measured with EMF detectors and dowsing rods. Mediums find the area overwhelmingly disturbing. The annual re-enactment of the "Come and Take It" battle at nearby Pioneer Village probably adds extra energy to the hauntings in the area.

Texas' Real Ghost Towns

Texas is the home of many haunted forts. The state also has many ghost towns with stories to tell. Some of them still have real ghosts.

Abandoned towns are sometimes haunted by the people who lived and died there. Abandoned cemeteries are even more likely to be haunted by people who don't want to be forgotten.

Fairland and Oak Hill are both known as haunted ghost towns.

Fairland was settled in the early 1850s, and named for its spectacular location. However, building stopped there during the Civil War when the economy of Texas economy suffered. Only about a hundred people lived there at its peak. Today, just a handful of people remain in the beautiful town of Fairland.

Fairland is located just south of the town of Burnet, Texas, in Hill Country. When you visit it, be sure to stop at the cemetery where markers date to the 1870s. Crownover Chapel is another must-see in the middle of town. It has been perfectly preserved and represents a typical church in a small nineteenth century Texas town.

To reach Fairland, travel south from Burnet to Farm Road 1855 where it intersects U.S. Highway 281. Fairland is between Burnet and Marble Falls.

Oak Hill was once a thriving agricultural community between Bastrop and Elgin, Texas. However, during World War II, the War Department announced their plans to build Camp Swift where the town was. By the middle of 1942, Oak Hill had been emptied, except for its cemetery.

At some point during the war, the War Department changed its mind. More than half of the acreage in Oak Hill was returned to its owners. The remaining land is still part of Camp Swift, and used by the National Guard.

The town is still largely deserted, but the cemetery is well worth a visit if you're a ghost hunter.

Oak Hill is on Farm Road 2336, northeast of the intersection with Texas State Highway 95.

Finding More Haunted Forts and Ghost Towns

At one time, Texas was dotted with forts. Each fort—whether it's still there or simply indicated on an historical map—has a story to tell, and most have at least one or two ghosts.

If you find a fort, you'll probably find a ghost story.

Likewise, many abandoned towns have a rich history of unfulfilled dreams, as well as brutal and violent episodes from Texas' early days. Any of these can lead to residual energy hauntings, as well as lingering ghosts.

To locate more ghosts, research the history of the surrounding area. Ask at the local historical society, the chamber of commerce, and the visitors center. Local Texas librarians are often fabulous resources for history and ghost stories.

Texas is a bottomless well of opportunities to encounter ghosts.

STRICTLY FOR A "GOOD SCARE"— AUSTIN'S NIGHTLY BAT DISPLAY

Congress Avenue Bridge may not be haunted, but it's a must-see attraction for people who enjoy a "good scare." The bridge provides an eerie display each night from mid-March to early November.

Austin is the home of North America's largest urban colony of bats. As many as 1.5 million Mexican free-tail bats emerge from beneath the Congress Avenue Bridge each night when they get hungry.

The bridge is at Congress Avenue, about ten blocks south of the State Capitol building.

During the day, the bats are concealed in crevices that were created in the bridge when it was reconstructed in 1980. The bats' chirping and crunching sounds can seem very creepy as they echo from nearby walls and paved paths.

Wooded viewing area next to the Congress Avenue Bridge.
Photo by the author.

Around dusk, the bats emerge in clusters as if choreographed. First, one section of the bridge is active, then the section next to it, and so on. The activity starts at one end of the bridge, usually the side nearest the Hyatt-Regency Hotel. Section by section, it progresses gradually to the other bank of the river nearest the Austin American-Statesman's Bat Observation Center.

The bats soar over the river for a few seconds and then take off in pursuit of food. It's an extraordinary sight, and best viewed from on top of the bridge or from viewing areas on either side of the river.

When the bats first began their nightly performances in 1980, the people of Austin were fascinated by this unusual sight. Fear gradually replaced the sense of novelty, and Bat Conservation International—an Austin-based group—launched an education program to protect the bats.

These bats are gentle and sophisticated animals that rid Austin of more than 10,000 pounds of insects—including mosquitoes and agricultural pests—each night. If you join the hundreds of people who watch for them nightly, you are in no danger, as long as you don't try to handle the bats. Like any wild animal, they can become defensive if you try to touch them or pick them up.

During the summer months, special bat-watchers' boat tours leave from the dock at the Hyatt-Regency Austin Hotel on Barton Springs Drive. Generally, the tours leave thirty minutes before sunset. Be certain to check their schedules ahead of time, and make reservations if recommended. This is a popular Austin attraction.

If you prefer to keep your feet on the ground, you can observe the bats from the Hyatt-Regency's Branchwater Lounge, which overlooks Town Lake. Or, enjoy a meal at T. G. I. Friday's at the Radisson Hotel & Suites, 111 E. Cesar Chavez Street, Austin; they have a large observation deck for bat-watchers.

The Austin American-Statesman's Bat Observation Center is at the southeast side of the Congress Avenue Bridge. There is an educational kiosk, and—on weekend evenings during the summer—Bat Interpreters from Bat Conservation International are on hand.

The Austin American-Statesman provides free car parking in their lot after six p.m. You'll also find free parking nearby at the Texas Department of Transportation parking lot, located on Riverside Drive.

The bats usually emerge shortly after sunset, but you can call the bat hotline at 512-416-5700 (Category 3636) for the latest flight times, or check the Bat Conservation International website at http://www.batcon.org/.

They fly each night no matter what the weather, but rain can disrupt their schedule.

The best months for viewing the bats are July and August. There are no picnic tables or other seating at the Bat Observation Center, so it's smart to bring a lawn chair or blanket to sit upon. Also, there are no rest rooms and no food sold at the site, but there are several nearby restaurants.

Over a million bats fly out from their roosts beneath the Congress Avenue Bridge.
Photo by the author.

If you watch the bats from on top of the bridge, be very careful of traffic. Most people gather below or near the bridge. If you do, be sure to wear a hat.

If you like bats, there are other even more dramatic locations within a comfortable driving distance of Austin.

Old Tunnel Wildlife Management Area

During its nightly display, the Old Tunnel Wildlife Management Area offers about twice as many bats as the Congress Avenue Bridge. It's an easy and direct drive, about seventy miles west of Austin.

The park contains 16.1 acres of beautiful land and nature trails, plus the abandoned railway tunnel that is home to as many as three million Mexican free-tail bats and about 3,000 cave myotis, a variety of colonial, cave dwelling bat. Unlike the Mexican free-tail bats which migrate each year, cave myotis hibernate during the winter and remain in central Texas.

There are two viewing areas, each with an information kiosk explaining more about bats. One viewing area is located at the top of the hill, and the other at the foot of it. Both are handicapped accessible.

The park is open for bat watching seven nights a week, and educational presentations are given Thursday through Sunday, from May to October.

The Old Tunnel WMA also has three picnic tables (not covered) and a two-stall self-composting restroom facility, but no running water. T-shirts, caps, posters, and resource books can be purchased during tour nights.

Emergence times can vary by as much as two hours. The mouth of the tunnel is too small for all of the bats to fly out at once. If the bat population is very large, they fly out of the tunnel earlier to give time for all the bats to hunt for food. If there are a lot of insects in the area, they can leave the tunnel later and still find plenty of food.

In the spring and summer, expect the bats to leave the tunnel as early as eight p.m. By August, they may fly at six-thirty p.m., and even earlier in September and October when the days are shorter.

Driving directions

On Highway 290, about half a mile east of Fredericksburg, look for a brown sign that says, "Old Tunnel Wildlife Area." Turn south on the Old San Antonio Road and drive ten and a half miles. The Old Tunnel Wildlife Management Area will be on the left as you approach the top of the hill.

For tours and emergence times, contact the Old Tunnel staff at (866) 978-2287.

Eckert James River Bat Cave Preserve

True bat enthusiasts will be thrilled by a trip to Mason County. It's among the world's top ten free-tailed bat sites, and Eckert James River Bat Cave Preserve houses as many as six to eight million bats each summer.

The Eckert James River Bat Cave Preserve is in Mason County, Texas, about two hours northwest of Austin. Each May, about four million pregnant female bats arrive at this cave.

Each pregnant bat will usually give birth to one pup in June or July, so the bat population may double by mid-summer. The babies can fly when they're about five weeks old.

Every night, an hour or two before sunset, you can hear the chirping and whirring sound of bats near the mouth of the limestone cave. Then, a stream of bats emerges. Soon, hundreds of hungry bats fly in a circle very low to the ground, followed by thousands and then millions more.

Listen carefully. Their initial chirping noises are soon replaced with the Dracula-like fluttering of wings. The noise can be disturbing as the living column of bats builds.

As their numbers increase, these hungry creatures become a dense tornado of bats, swirling hundreds of feet into the sky. Once the bats reach the top of the funnel-like formation, they fly off in different directions to search for food.

This performance lasts about an hour, and it is a magnificent and eerie sight. Bring your camera; it's a good idea to use a tripod when the light becomes very low.

The Bat Cave Preserve is located at James River Road in Mason County, about eighteen miles southwest of the town of Mason. It is open from mid-May to early October for interpretive tours between six and nine p.m., Thursday through Sunday. There is a small admission fee; children age five and under are free. The caves are not wheelchair accessible, and baby strollers aren't recommended either.

Some sunrise tours are also offered, when the bats return to the cave each morning.

In the early 1900s, bat guano was regularly harvested from the cave and sold as fertilizer. In 1990, the Eckert family donated the cave to The Nature Conservancy. That guarantees that the public will always be able to enjoy the land around it.

Today, the Preserve land covers about eight acres. Bat Conservation International and the Texas Nature Conservancy manage the it jointly.

Driving directions

Follow Highway 87 about one mile to FM 1723 and turn right. (FM 1723 is before the city park. If you reach the park, turn around.) Follow FM 1723 for about two and a half miles to FM 2389.

Follow FM 2389 for about five miles—including two bridges over the Llano River—until you reach James River Road, where you will turn right and drive a little over eight miles. You're about halfway there when the paving ends and changes to a dirt road.

Continue on the James River Road to the James River crossing. Before you reach the James River, you will pass the Dalton Woods turnoff on your right. Although it's paved, do not turn onto it; remain on the dirt road.

When you arrive at the James River, remain on the road and drive slowly across (and through) the river. Drive close to the small waterfalls, but keep them on your right side. Just to the left of the falls is where the water level is most constant. The river bottom is hard rock and a little slick at times, but—unless there is flooding—the river can be crossed.

It's smart to check weather conditions and James River water levels ahead of time. One resource is the Mason Cave Steward, at (325) 347-5970.

Continue along the James River Road about a half mile until the road makes a sharp turn to the left; the gate to the Eckert James River Bat Cave Preserve will be on the right. Follow that road to the parking lot.

More Bat Observation Areas

Other Texas areas where you can see bats include Kickapoo Cavern State Park in Kinney County near Bracketville; Devil's Sinkhole State Natural Area in Edwards County near Rocksprings (open only by special arrangements); and Caprock Canyons State Park in Briscoe County east of Silverton.

The world's largest gathering of Mexican free-tail bats is at Bracken Bat Cave & Nature Preserve, near San Antonio, Texas. Each summer, as many as twenty million bats gather there. However, this site is open only on select nights, and usually limited to Bat Conservation International members. Contact BCI for more information, at (512) 327-9721.

These bat displays may not be ghostly, but you're certain to be reminded of Dracula. It's an experience that will send a chill up the spine of the most intrepid ghost hunter.

APPENDIX

THE TOP TEN PLACES TO FIND GHOSTS

No matter where you are, certain locations are usually haunted. These sites don't always have ghosts, but they're the best places to start when you're looking for unreported visitors from beyond the grave.

Theatres

Ghosts frequent places where people have performed on stage. These include movie theatres that were once performance halls.

There are three kinds of ghosts at these locations:

First, at least one actor who is still seen on or near the stage.

Second, a stagehand lingers backstage, usually around the lighting or the curtain controls.

Finally, someone appears towards the back of the hall, especially during rehearsals. He or she almost always smokes a cigarette that people can smell, or they'll see the smoke or the burning ember.

Battlegrounds

Almost every battleground has some residual energy from the violent and tragic deaths that occurred there. Some battlegrounds are actually haunted by the spirits of the men and women who died there, too. Between Texas' battles for independence, Indian attacks, and Civil War conflicts, you'll find many locations with ghost stories... and real ghosts.

Cemeteries

It's a cliché but a true one: Ghosts haunt cemeteries. Modern graves—burials that occurred less than fifty years ago—are rarely haunted for very long.

For the most powerful hauntings, look for graves that are at least a hundred years old. Only a few are haunted, but you'll find elevated EMF levels at many of graves, especially if they're unmarked.

Colleges

Almost every college or university reports at least one ghost. Most also report poltergeist phenomena. The performing arts center is often the most haunted location on campus. In Austin, the University of Texas campus is probably the most haunted college.

Summer Camps

Most camps—especially Scout camps—have a ghost or two. Usually, these are benevolent ghosts of former camp counselors or the camp manager. An aroma of perfume or pipe smoke is usually reported, related to someone who worked there.

Very Old, Large Homes and Buildings

Like most ancient castles, many very old, large buildings have ghosts. In an older home, a woman who lived there lingers to be sure that the house and its occupants remain safe. She usually wears a green dress.

Another ghost is mad and lurks in the attic, basement, or an outbuilding. A variation on this is a ghost in the nearby woods or a field next to an old homestead. These hauntings are almost predictable.

However, in Austin, you simply need to visit homes and buildings constructed by Abner Cook using bricks with the Shoal Creek Curse. Many are listed in this book, from the Texas Governor's Mansion to the UT Tower.

Old Hotels

Many hotels are haunted by the same people who visited them in life. They're usually happy ghosts who return to relax and enjoy themselves.

Classic haunted spots in hotels include the top floor, the elevator, and the lobby. This is true of the Driskill Hotel, Austin's most haunted and elegant hotel, and a favorite destination for visiting ghost hunters.

Around Austin, this category of haunting extends to former brothels. In the late nineteenth century, dozens of feisty, independent-minded madams owned "boarding houses" around downtown Austin. Today, these sites are often clubs, bars, and restaurants in the entertainment and warehouse districts of Austin. And, most of them have great ghost stories to share.

Hospitals, Retirement Homes, Morgues and Funeral Parlors

As you'd expect, some people aren't willing to leave the last place where they were seen and called by name. However, if these sites are still in use, they're usually off-limits to ghost hunters.

Instead, look for former locations of these kinds of buildings. They're usually haunted by perplexed and sometimes angry ghosts.

Around Austin, there are probably hundreds of unreported ghosts. If you follow these suggestions, you'll find even more ghosts than are included in these pages.

Row of crypts. *Photo by the author.*

GUIDELINES FOR GHOST HUNTERS

Real ghost photo. *Photo by the author.*

1. **Use common sense**. If your "gut feeling" indicates that you're in danger, leave immediately. Ghost hunting shouldn't be dangerous, and it shouldn't be an endurance test, either.

2. **Never trespass**. If the site has "no trespassing" signs or looks as if it's closed, don't go in. Don't risk arrest.

3. **Take a friend with you** when you go ghost hunting. Never go to a quiet or deserted site alone, and never explore risky neighborhoods on your own.

4. **Dress for the setting**. Sturdy shoes are vital, especially if you're outdoors, or if you have to run to get away from a ghost.

5. Before visiting a location after dark, **see it in the daylight** to check for hazards, and things that might confuse you in lower light conditions.

6. **Never joke around cemeteries or other haunted locations.** That seems to offend the ghosts, and they can retaliate. Or, they may become obstinate and refuse to manifest.

7. Ghosts generally don't look "dead." Few ghosts appear as full figure apparitions. When they talk, it's often a garbled whisper. That's why we **record their "voices"** to study more carefully, later. (See "EVP" in the Glossary section of this book.)

8. **Interact with the ghosts as if they're alive.** Be polite; they usually consider the location their personal property. Don't command them to manifest in a specific way. Unless they're ghosts of actors, they won't usually perform for anyone on cue.

9. **Ghosts don't follow you home.** If you're troubled by unwanted thoughts or feel uneasy after a ghost hunt, call a friend. Play your favorite music. Watch a funny TV show

or movie. If dark or scary thoughts continue, consult your minister or spiritual advisor.

10. **Keep detailed notes** about your ghost hunts. Later, you'll find these notes very helpful, especially if you want to re-visit those haunted sites.

FIONA'S TIPS FOR TAKING GREAT GHOST PHOTOS

Avoid lens flares. Don't point the lens towards the sun, lights, a full moon, or any reflective surface. At least 80% of the orb photos that I review are clearly reflections from shiny surfaces or lights that are in the frame of the photo or just outside it.

Don't take pictures in high humidity or rain. Moisture in the air can result in dozens—even hundreds—of orbs in a single photo. If you see too many orbs in your pictures, or many very tiny orbs among larger ones, they're probably from rain or high humidity.

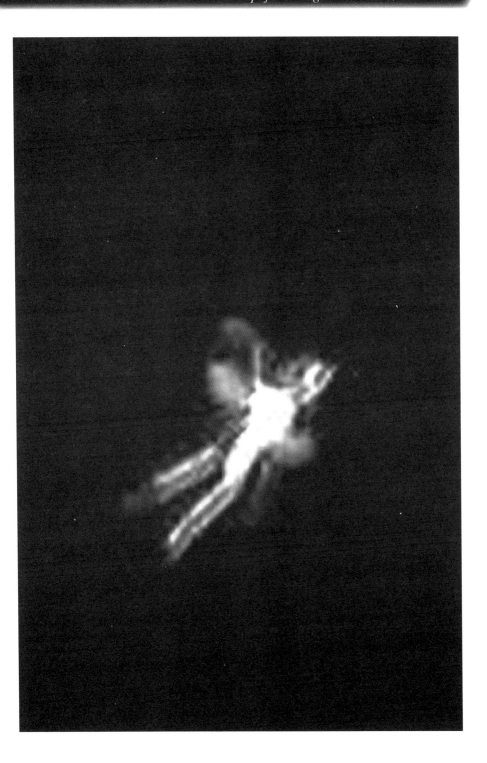

Watch out for bugs. Your ghost hunting companion should watch for insects in front of the camera as you take pictures. Both pictures shown here on pages 199 and 200 are bugs.

Genuine orbs are almost perfectly round. If the orb is oval, irregularly shaped, or has blurry borders, it's probably an insect.

Avoid smoke. Tests show that smoke from cigarettes causes fewer eerie effects than many researchers guessed. However, even when you can't see or smell smoke, if someone has been smoking nearby, it can still cause misty shapes in your photos.

Keep your camera strap and your hair out of the way. Some people might call the photo on page 202 a "vortex." We know that it's a camera strap. (The solitary orb is real.)

The picture on page 203 may look like traveling orbs. Those lines actually represent strands of hair.

Always take two photos in a row, moving as little as possible between the clicks of the camera's shutter. If your picture shows an actual anomaly, it will usually appear in only one photo. If it looks almost exactly the same (size, brightness, location) in both pictures, it's probably a reflection, or a hovering insect.

Save all of your pictures until you've seen at least a dozen with orbs and anomalies. Until you know what you're looking for, you may not realize how many anomalies are in your photos.

If you use a film camera, the photo lab may adjust the contrast to prevent the orbs (and other anomalies) from "spoiling" your photos. Sometimes, you have to study the negatives to find the orbs.

I've taken hundreds of photos that clearly show orbs on the negative but those same orbs are easily overlooked on the print. It took years of practice to spot these orbs without referring to the negatives.

When you realize how faint some orbs are, you'll probably find dozens of overlooked "ghosts" in your pictures.

Right:
Haunted headstones. *Photo by the author.*

GLOSSARY OF
COMMON GHOST HUNTING TERMS

There are many words that ghost hunters use in reference to ghosts and haunted places. You're probably familiar with most of these words, but some may be new or have different meanings when they refer to haunted places.

Afterlife

One of several terms used interchangeably to refer to life after death. The word "afterlife" has been used since 1615, and is generic enough to use in almost any setting and culture. Other popular terms include "crossing over," "the Otherworld," and "the other side."

Most ghost hunters avoid specific religious terms such as "heaven" and "the Summerland" when discussing ghosts, hauntings, and an afterlife.

Aliens

Visitors from other planets. We differentiate aliens from visitors that live in parallel worlds, the Otherworld, or what's generally characterized as the afterlife. Some ghost hunters believe in UFOs and aliens; others don't. Generally, ghost hunters don't mix the two studies.

Anomaly

Something that is out of place and unexplained. In paranormal studies, this word refers to any phenomena that we cannot explain. Example: A lens flare in a photo is not an anomaly if you can see the light source that created it. A orb that cannot be explained is an anomaly.

Apparition

Since the early seventeenth century, this word has referred to a ghost that seems to have material substance. If it appears in any physical form, including a vapor-like image, it may be called an apparition.

Banshee

From the Irish, bean sidhe, meaning female spirit. Most families with Irish ancestors have at least one banshee story if you do enough research, but many people are reluctant to discuss this subject. Her wail does not always mean death. She does not cause anyone to die. She's generally not a ghost.

Clearing, or Space Clearing

This is a process of ridding an area of lingering unpleasant energy. It does not "kill" a ghost. Space clearing may encourage ghosts to cross over, or at least leave the haunted location.

Immediately after a space clearing, ghosts can be noisier or more hostile than usual. An effective space clearing may take three to five days to work. In the most haunted settings, it's usually necessary to repeat the space clearing several times.

Demons

Historically, this term has included deceased individuals. However, since the early eighteenth century, the word "demon" usually refers to an evil spirit, sometimes more powerful than man, but less than Deity. Today, we generally do not use this term to indicate a deceased human being. The female demon, very rarely mentioned, is a demoness.

Demons and possessions are treated like UFOs and aliens. That is, most ghost hunters have an opinion about them, but they rarely discuss them in connection with hauntings. The "Amityville Horror" is one noted exception where the story seemed to include both ghosts and possessions.

Ghosts generally do not attempt to take over a living body. In most cases, they believe that they're still alive and—in their minds—each has his or her own body. They're not interested in anyone else's.

Doppelganger

A concept made popular in the early nineteenth century, especially by Shelley and Byron. The doppelganger is the apparition, or double, of a living person.

This may be paranormal phenomenon, but it's not a ghost. It does not forecast anything tragic.

Dowsing rods

These are usually single rods, split rods, or L-shaped wires or twigs. Some people dowse with pendulums, too. They're popularly used to locate water and oil wells, and to measure energy levels of many kinds. For ghost research, we usually use two L-shaped rods.

In ghost hunting, the investigator loosely carries one rod in each hand, and watches the movement of the rods. When the rods cross or splay wide apart, it usually indicates a haunted location.

It's easy to make your own dowsing rods from coat hanger wire. Cut the wire near the top, and again at the opposite end of the lower section. Do this with two different coat hangers to create two dowsing rods.

You can also purchase ready-made dowsing rods. Be certain that they're long enough for ghost research; the 16-inch length is very popular. Look for dowsing tools that glow in the dark. They're especially useful for ghost hunting.

Hold each one loosely in your hands with your arms extended or your elbows bent at a right angle. The rods should be pointed straight ahead of you, and able to swing on their own.

If the rods are drifting, this could be from the normal movement of your body. However, in haunted places, the pull on the rods is strong and cannot be mistaken for a casual, unconscious movement of your hands.

When you step out of the haunted area, the rods return to their original position.

Some researchers successfully use dowsing rods to find unmarked graves. With practice, it's possible to use the rods to detect other information about the body in the grave and the spirit that may haunt the site.

Ectoplasm

Often referred to as "ecto," this is the physical residue of psychic energy. It's the basis for "slime" used in the Ghostbusters movies. Ectoplasm can be seen by the naked eye, and is best viewed in dark settings, since it is translucent and tends to glow. It is very unusual.

Researchers often describe it as a vivid, X-Files kind of lime green. It usually fades from sight gradually.

EMF

The initials stand for Electro Magnetic Field, or Electro Magnetic Frequency. In the broadest terms, EMF is a combination of electrical and magnetic fields. You'll find EMF around power sources, fuse boxes, electrical outlets, computer monitors, microwave ovens, etc.

It's smart to study EMF so that you'll recognize the normal sources of elevated EMF readings.

Constant, clearly defined EMF fields usually have a logical explanation.

Unexplained EMF fields may indicate something paranormal. EMF fields can be measured with various tools, including an EMF meter or a hiking compass.

Entity

An entity is any being, including people, animals, and ghosts. It can also refer to aliens, faeries, mystical beasts, and a wide range of paranormal creatures. If you use this term—and many ghost hunters do—be sure that others understand your context.

ESP

ESP is the abbreviation for Extra Sensory Perception. It means the ability to perceive things beyond the usual five senses of smell, hearing, touch, taste, and sight.

Although these perceptions may be interpreted as sounds or sights, experienced ghost hunters can usually tell the difference between normal detection with the five senses, and things detected with the "sixth sense" or psychic abilities.

EVP

Electronic Voice Phenomena, or the recording of unexplained voices, usually in haunted settings. Sometimes the voices are heard during the investigation. More often, the voices are whispers, understood only when a sound recording is processed, filtered, and amplified with a computer.

When people first recorded EVP, they insisted on total silence so normal noises and talking wouldn't be confused with EVP. More recently, people have deliberately included sounds such as normal talking, white noise, and so on. Some researchers believe that ghosts may need ambient noise to create their own sounds and speech.

Most researchers use digital recorders to save EVP. Once the researcher is at home, he or she uses a computer program to filter out everyday noises, such as airplanes and passing cars. The recording may need to be speeded up or slowed down, or a range of sounds magnified above others.

Faeries

Beings that live in the Otherworld or Underworld, parallel to our world and not far from it. Many researchers who readily accept the reality of ghosts don't believe in faeries. Similar to the subject of aliens and UFOs, it's best to keep faerie research clearly separated from your ghost hunting.

Fear

Most ghost hunters have a healthy respect for ghosts and paranormal phenomena. Many ghost hunters enjoy a "good scare." However, if you feel genuinely alarmed or frightened while ghost hunting, it's prudent to leave that location. It may have been your imagination, but there may be something (or someone) truly dangerous nearby.

Ghost hunting should always be interesting, and sometimes entertaining. If it's not, you may be at risk. Ghost hunting should never become a "dare" or an endurance test.

If you're truly frightened in any setting—haunted or not—leave immediately. If this happens regularly when you're ghost hunting, choose a different hobby.

Ghost

A sentient entity or spirit that visits or lingers in our world, after he or she lived among us as a human being. We've also seen evidence of ghostly animals and pets.

Ghost hunters generally use other terms for other beings such as aliens and faeries.

Ghoul

This word has been mistakenly used to mean a ghost. "Ghoul" comes from Middle Eastern lore, where it may refer to an evil spirit that robs graves.

Haunted

Describes a setting where ghosts, poltergeists, and/or residual energy seem to produce significant paranormal activity. The word "haunt" originally meant to frequent.

Hollow Hill

Hollow Hill is the name of Fiona Broome's ghost hunting website!

http://www.HollowHill.com/

It is one of the oldest and most trusted ghost-related websites online.

Medium

This word usually refers to something in the middle, relative to size or duration.

In ghost hunting, it means anyone who is able to convey communications from departed spirits. That is, the person is able to maintain a position between the world of the living and those who've crossed over, and talk with (or for) those on the other side.

This term was popularized in the mid nineteenth century and is often used interchangeably with the word "psychic." (Compare that definition in this glossary.)Some people call themselves psychic mediums because they can communicate with the other side, but also sense other paranormal energy and/or work with ESP.

Occult

From the Latin, meaning something that is concealed or covered. Since the sixteenth century, it has meant anything that is mysterious. Today in America, it generally refers to magical, mystical and experimental studies.

Orb

An orb is a round, whitish or pastel-colored translucent area in photos. Generally, these are perfectly circular, not oval. Many researchers believe that they represent spirits or ghosts.

If you're using a digital camera, it's important to differentiate between an area of broken pixels (called an "artifact") and the translucent, circular image that is an orb.

Also, any reflective surface or light source can create a lens flare that looks like an orb. When taking photos, note glass, shiny metal, reflective signs, polished surfaces such as tables and headstones, and lights.

In most cases, ghost hunters do not see orbs when they're at a haunted site. Usually, orbs show up only in photos. They are the most common evidence for hauntings.

Critics often dismiss orbs as lens flares and artifacts. However, unexplained orbs often appear at haunted sites. They're rarely in photos at locations that aren't haunted.

Ouija

From the French and German words for "yes," this is a spelling board used with a planchette. The device is intended to communicate with and through the spirit world, obtaining answers to questions.

Generally, we don't recommend them on serious ghost investigations. Some people are vehemently opposed to Ouija boards. The biggest problem is that researchers can't tell who is really moving the planchette. Even if it is a ghost, the spirit could be playing a prank or lying; the information from Ouija boards is unreliable for ghost research.

Paranormal

The prefix, "para" indicates something that is irregular, faulty, or operating outside the usual boundaries. So, "paranormal" refers to anything outside the realm and experiences that we consider normal.

Parapsychology

The study of mental abilities and effects outside the usual realm of psychology. Parapsychology includes the study of ESP, ghosts, luck, psychokinesis, and other paranormal phenomena.

Pendulum

A small weight at the end of a cord or chain that is usually about six to ten inches long. The movement of the weight, when uninfluenced by other factors, can be used to detect areas of paranormal energy.

Poltergeist

From the German meaning "noisy ghost," this term has been in use since the early nineteenth century to mean a spirit that makes noise, or otherwise plays pranks... usually annoying. Unlike other ghosts, poltergeists can move from one location to another, following the person they've chosen to torment.

Many psychologists believe that poltergeists are not ghosts at all, but some form of psychokinesis or remote activity.

Portal

Literally, a doorway or gate, this term suggests a specific location through which spirits enter and leave our world. When there are multiple phenomena in a confined area, such as an abundance of unexplained orbs, some people call this a "ghost portal."

Possession

When an entity attempts to take control of a body that does not belong to them, it's called a possession.

In ghost hunting, this phenomenon is rare, but some psychics and mediums allow ghosts to speak through them. Sometimes, this can enable the living to communicate directly with the ghost and help him or her to cross over.

In extreme cases, a spirit can maliciously attempt to take over an unwilling person's body. Most ghost hunters will never witness this kind of possession, though it's a popular scene in horror movies. Unwilling possession is often linked to demonic activity.

Proof

There is no "proof" of ghosts when someone is a committed skeptic. People who won't believe in ghosts find other explanations for all scientific evidence of hauntings.

A profound, personal encounter with a ghost or the unexplainable is the only way to change someone's mind about haunted places.

Protection

Some researchers use objects, rituals, routines, tactics, or specific processes to protect themselves against ghostly, demonic, or paranormal intrusions and effects. This is a personal matter and rarely discussed during a ghost hunt.

When you go on a ghost hunt, it's generally smart to carry something that you feel may protect you from evil. Most ghost hunters wear a small cross, Star of David, pentacle, or other religious jewelry. They often conceal it under clothing, or wear it as a ring, earrings, or on a bracelet where it won't be noticed.

Carrying a very big, heavy Bible, an intimidating (and very visible) athame, or a large religious icon is usually considered excessive.

Psi

"Psi" or "psy" is a popular term used to mean any psychic phenomena or psychic abilities. This term is sometimes inclusive of paranormal disturbances as well.

Psychic

From the Greek word meaning of the soul, or of life (Paul used it in the Bible, I Cor ii, 14), this word usually refers to the world outside the domain of physical law.

"Psychic" can relate to the spirit or the mind, depending upon the context. When someone is described as a psychic, it usually means that he or she is able to perceive things that are outside traditional physical laws and perceptions.

Psychical

A British term used as an adjective or adverb, for what Americans call "psychic."

Psychokinesis or Psycho Kinesis

To move something with the powers of one's mind, alone. It may be a factor in some hauntings, and particularly in poltergeist phenomena. It's usually called "PK." (Also see telekinesis.)

Residual Energy

Many ghost hunters believe that emotionally-charged events leave an imprint or residue on the physical objects nearby.

What distinguishes residual energy from an active haunting is that the energy/impressions repeat consistently, as if on a tape loop. The energy level may increase or decrease, but the content remains the same with each manifestation.

By contrast, in an active haunting, the ghost may respond to environmental stimuli and direct contact.

Sixth Sense

Since normal phenomena are detected with the five senses (smell, taste, touch, hearing, and sight), anything that you experience outside those five senses may be categorized as a sixth sense. Usually, this indicates to psychic detection or ESP.

Since M. Knight Shyamalan's movie of the same name, people usually think that the sixth sense refers primarily to seeing ghosts. In reality, few people see ghosts as full figures or living people.

In ghost hunting, the sixth sense can include everything from the ability to hear ghosts whispering, to an internal visual image from the past, or even a "creepy feeling" that can't be explained.

Sparkles

This paranormal visual effect is sometimes described as the sparkle of embers falling immediately after a fireworks display. These small, sparkling lights usually occur no closer to the camera than ten feet. They are often twenty to fifty feet away, or more. Sparkles are seen during, and especially immediately after, the flash on a camera is used.

Even the most vivid sparkles will not show up on film. They are paranormal phenomena.

"Sparkles" is a proprietary term developed in the 1990s by Fiona Broome during research for Hollow Hill. Other researchers have adopted the term to describe this unique phenomenon.

Spirit

This word comes from the Latin, meaning that which breathes. It means that which animates life, or the soul of the being.

Table Tapping, Table Tipping

A method to communicate with spirits. Usually, several people sit around a table with their hands on it, or holding hands on top of the table. Then, they ask the spirits to reply to communicate by tapping on the table, perhaps once for yes and twice for no.

Others are successful asking the ghosts to lift the table very slightly to show that they are present. Then, the ghosts may tap their replies, move a Ouija-type platen, or use some other means to communicate with movement around the table.

Tarot

The history of the Tarot deck is still unclear. However, since its use in fourteenth century Italy, "Tarot" refers to playing cards that are also used for fortune-telling or divination.

Telekinesis

From a Greek word meaning any motion that is activated from a distance. Technically, this could describe a remote-controlled toy boat, so most people use the word psychokinesis for ghost research.

Vortex

Since the time of Descartes, this has indicated the rotation of cosmic energy around a central point or axis. Beginning in the mid-nineteenth century, the word "vortex" has meant any whirling movement of energy or particles.

Some people use this term to explain lines or narrow cylinders that appear highlighted in ghost photos.

ACKNOWLEDGMENTS

There are so many people to thank for their help and support as I researched and wrote this book. Trying to list them all is perilous, because I'm certain to leave someone out... and probably several people. I appreciate the help of everyone who has been part of this process, whether I remember to list you here or not.

First, I am indebted to my editors, Tina and Dinah, for their encouragement as this book took unexpected and interesting turns.

Thanks also to my family—and especially HT—for continued enthusiasm for my projects, and patience when I've needed extra time for ghost research.

Special thanks to:

Beth Krauss and the staff of the Austin Visitor Information Center, for interesting tours and helpful background information.

Bill Stein and Tonya Britton of Columbus, Texas, for inspiring stories and perspectives. Thanks also to Peggy Sanford for insights related to Native history and the innate energy of the land.

Brian Chabot, who continually opens new ways to research ghosts.

Charlotte and the staff at the Katy, Texas LDS Family History Library, for steady encouragement.

Dale Flatt of Save Austin Cemeteries, who dropped everything to share insights into Oakwood Cemetery and other important landmarks.

Elmo Johnson of Texas Paranormal Researchers, and the many members of that group, for camaraderie on research trips.

Erin Shoemate of NeedCoffee.com deserves special thanks for getting me away from the keyboard when I most needed it, and for inspiration in general.

Dr. Frank Gordon for profound spiritual insights.

Grant Wilson and Jason Hawes of The Atlantic Paranormal Society (TAPS) for their sincerity, humor, and sense of perspective when this book neared completion.

Mary Beth Temple and M. J. Plaster, for continued encouragement as a writer.

Pete Haviland of Lone Star Spirits Paranormal investigations, who generously shared leads to several stories in this book.

Shadow of Dragon*Con for a full-day discussion that opened many doors to alternative views of ghosts and hauntings.

Vernon Pope whose enthusiasm for Austin's Ripper lore supported me through that chapter.

Diana G. Gallagher for her thoughtful questions about ghost hunting, and her insights into hauntings and magic.

And, my most profound thanks to the many Austin business owners and staff who paused to share personal stories with me—on or off the record—to enrich this book for readers.

BIBLIOGRAPHY

Abbott, Olyve H. *Ghosts in the Graveyard: Texas Cemetery Tales*. Plano, TX: Republic of Texas Press, 2002.

"AGS Travis County Completed Cemeteries." *Austin Texas Genealogical Society*. 29 Apr. 2006. Austin Texas Genealogical Society. 29 Apr. 2006<http://www.austintxgensoc.org/cemeteries/cemcomp.html>.

"Alamo Survivor Susannah Dickinson." *Sons of Dewitt Colony Texas*. 2001. Texas A&M University. 2 Apr. 2006<http://www.tamu.edu/ccbn/dewitt/sdickinson.htm>.

Alexander, Drury Blakely. *The Governor's Mansion of Texas: a Historic Tour*. Austin: Friends of the Governor's Mansion, 1985.

"The Arno Nowotny Building." *The University of Texas at Austin*. 14 Mar. 2006<http://www.utexas.edu/academic/uip/inside/arno.html>.

"Austin Ghost Hunters Meetup Group message board."
   Meetup. 5 Jan. 2006. Meetup.com. 5 Jan. 2006<http://
   ghosts.meetup.com/52/boards/>.

"Austin History: A Brief History." *KLRU-TV*. 13 Mar.
   2006<http://www.klru.org/austinhistory/history.html>.

"Austin's Guy Town." *History House*. 7 Mar. 2006<http://
   www.historyhouse.com/in_history/guy_town/ >.

"Austin, Texas." *Wikipedia*. 13 Sept. 2006. 13 Sept.
   2006<http://en.wikipedia.org/wiki/Austin%2C_Texas>.

Avila, Alfred. *Mexican Ghost Tales of the Southwest*. Houston:
   Pinata Books, 1984.

"Battle of Gonzales." *Sons of Dewitt Colony, Texas*. Texas
   A&M University. 14 Mar. 2006<http://www.tamu.edu/
   ccbn/dewitt/batgon.htm>.

Bear, Jacci Howard. "Architect Abner Cook - Greek Revival
   in Austin, Texas." *About.com*. 10 June 2006<http://
   austin.about.com/cs/architecture/p/abner_cook.htm>.

—. "Austin, TX - Abner Cook (1814 - 1884)." *About.com*. 8
   June 2006<http://austin.about.com/cs/architecture/p/
   abner_cook.htm>.

Bell, Bob Boze. "Ben Thompson & King Fisher vs Joe Foster & Billy Sims Classic Gunfight." *True West Magazine*. 4 July 2006. 13 Mar. 2006<http://www.twmag. com/classic-gunfights/classic-forewarned_03_06.htm>.

Bicknell, Tom. "The Proper Sort of a Person to become Marshall." *Images of Yorkshire*. 7 Mar. 2006<http://www. imagesofyorkshire.co.uk/famous_people/ben_thompson/ ben_thompson_marshall.htm>.

Biographical Encyclopedia of Texas. New York, New York: Southern Pub. Co., 1880. *The Portal to Texas History*. University of North Texas Libraries. 5 June 2006<http://texashistory.unt.edu/permalink/meta-pth-5827>.

Blackie. "Re: Dudley & Bob topics!" *KLBJ-FM Forums - Austin Fact*. 19 Apr. 2006. KLBJ FM. 3 July 2006<http:// forums.klbjfm.com/index.php?showforum=19>.

Blevins, Don. *From Angels to Hellcats: Legendary Texas Women*. Missoula, Montana: Mountain Press Publishing Company, 2001.

Boon, Mathilde E., and Lambrecht Kok. *Don't Mess with Texas!* Leiden, the Netherlands: Coulomb Press Leyden, 2005.

Brewer, J. Mason. *Dog Ghosts and Other Texas Negro Folk Tales*. Austin: University of Texas Press, 1958.

Britton, Tonya. "Re: Columbus Cemetery tour." E-mail to Fiona Broome. 3 Mar. 2006.

Butler, Wayne. "Milwood History." *Milwood Neighborhood Association*. Milwood Neighborhood Association. 24 Mar. 2006<http://www.milwoodna.com/index. php?menu=dat/m_hood.html&main=dat/hood.html>.

"Casebook: Jack the Ripper." *Casebook: Jack the Ripper*. 2006. 7 July 2006<http://www.casebook.org/index. html>.

Chapman, Betty T. "Women broke down barriers to own businesses in Houston." *Bizwomen*. 20 Sept. 2004. Houston Business Journal. 2 Apr. 2006<http://houston. bizjournals.com/bizwomen/houston/content/story. html?id=995664>.

Choate, Leigh Haney. "RE: FW: Info for upcoming book...?" E-mail to Fiona Broome. 29 June 2006.

Choron, James L. "Chilling Tales of Ghostly Experiences at the Alamo." *Texas Escapes Online Magazine*. 2006. 8 July 2006<http://www.texasescapes.com/Paranormal/Alamo-Ghosts.htm>.

Christensen, Jo-Anne. *Ghost Stories of Texas*. Edmonton, AB; Auburn, WA: Lone Line Publishers, 2001.

"Coke-Davis Dispute (January 1874)." *Lone Star Junction*. 1996. 7 Mar. 2006<http://http://www.lsjunction.com/events/cokedavs.htm>.

Coleman, Elaine. *Texas Haunted Forts*. Plano, Texas: Wordware Publishing, Incorporated, 2001.

"Colorado County District Court Records, Criminal Cause File Index 1837 - 1930." *The Townsend Society*. Townsend Society. 24 July 2006<http://www.townsendsociety.org/Members_Only/VitalRecords/TX/>.

"Colorado County Obituaries 'Stafford.'" *Rootsweb.com*. 24 July 2006<http://www.rootsweb.com/~txcolora/obits/obitsstafford.htm>.

"Columbus City Cemetery, Colorado County, Texas." *Rootsweb.com*. 7 Mar. 2006<http://www.rootsweb.com/~txcolora/cemeteries/columbuscitycem.htm>.

Curtis, Kiesha. "History of the Residence Halls at the University of Texas at Austin." *University of Texas: Division of Housing and Food Service.* 1 Mar. 2006. University of Texas at Austin. 1 Mar. 2006<http://www. utexas.edu/student/housing/index.php?site=8>.

Custer, Elizabeth Bacon. *Tenting On the Plains, Or, General Custer in Kansas and Texas.* Norman, OK: University of Oklahoma Press, 1994. *Net Library.*OCLC. 14 Mar. 2006<http://www.netlibrary.com/>.

Dobie, J. Frank. *I'll Tell You a Tale—An Anthology.* Austin: University of Texas Press, 1984.

Eckhardt, Charley F. *Tales of bad men, bad women, and bad places: four centuries of Texas outlawry.* Lubbock, Texas: Texas Tech University Press, 1999.

"Elegance on the frontier." *Neill-Cochran House Museum.* Neill-Cochran House Museum. 1 Mar. 2006<http:// www.neill-cochranmuseum.org/history.htm>.

"Episode 7." *Haunted Texas Vacations: The Complete Ghostly Guide.* The Armadillo Podcast. 27 Oct. 2005. Transcript. *Phenix Rising (blog).* 7 Apr. 2006 http://phenixrising. typepad.com/the_armadillo_podcast/2005/10/episode_ 7_.html.

Fehrenbach, T. R. *Lone Star: A History of Texas and the Texans.* New York: MacMillan, 1968.

Feit, Rachel. "Guy Town." *Texas Beyond History.* 1 Oct. 2001. University of Texas at Austin. 7 Mar. 2006<http://www. texasbeyondhistory.net/guytown/index.html>.

Fenster, Julic. *America's Grand Hotels.* Cold Spring Harbor, New York: Open Road Publishing, 1998.

Flatt, Dale. Personal interview. 26 Mar. 2006.

"Genealogy and Family History Records." *Ancestry Library Edition.* ProQuest Information and Learning. Church of Jesus Christ of Latter-Day Saints, Katy, TX. 22 Aug. 2006<http://ancestrylibrary.proquest.com/>.

"Ghosts of the Alamo in San Antonio, Texas." *Legends of America—Lone Star Legends.* 2006. 10 Aug. 2006<http:// www.legendsofamerica.com/TX-AlamoGhosts.html>.

Gibson, Elizabeth R. *The Wild, Wild West.* 2 Nov. 2005. 15 Mar. 2006<http://members.aol.com/Gibson0817/>.

Greaney, Devin, and Cindy Widner. "Bygone Buildings: There Are Ghost Towns Hidden Right Here in Boomtown." *The Austin Chronicle* 26 Jan. 2001. 28 Feb. 2006<http://www.austinchronicle.com/gyrobase/Issue/ story?oid=oid%3A80328>.

Hafertepe, Kenneth. "Cook, Abner Hugh." Handbook
of Texas Online. 6 June 2001. Texas State Historical
Association. 14 Mar. 2006<http://www.tsha.utexas.edu/
handbook/online/articles/CC/fco46.html>.

Harvey, Bill. *Texas cemeteries: the resting places of famous,
infamous, and just plain interesting Texans.* Austin, Texas:
University of Texas Press, 2003.

"Haunted Texas Towns - Austin." *Lone Star Spirits.* 2006. 12
Mar. 2006<http://www.lonestarspirits.org/hauntaustin.
html>.

"Haunted Texas Towns - Austin." *Lone Star Spirits
Paranormal Investigations.* 2006. 13 Aug. 2006<http://
www.lonestarspirits.org/hauntaustin.html>.

Haviland, Peter James. "Austin quotes." E-mail to Fiona
Broome. 30 July 2006.

—. Telephone interview. 30 July 2006.

Hinton, Don Allon. "Columbus, Texas." *Handbook of Texas
Online.* June 2001. Texas State Historical Association. 24
July 2006<http://www.tsha.utexas.edu/handbook/online/
articles/CC/hgc12.html>.

"Historical Markers - City of Columbus." *Welcome ot the City of Columbus, Texas.* 24 July 2006<http://www.columbustexas.net/markers.htm>.

Humphrey, David C. *Austin: A history of the capital city.* Austin, Texas: Texas State Historical Association, 1997.

—. *Austin: An Ilustrated History.* Northridge, CA: Windsor Publications, 1985.

—. "Prostitution." *Handbook of Texas Online.* June 2001. Texas State Historical Association. 14 Mar. 2006<http://www.tsha.utexas.edu/handbook/online/articles/PP/jbp1.html>.

Jameson, W. C. *Buried Treasures of Texas: Legends of Outlaw Loot, Pirate Hoards, Buried Mines, Ingots in Lakes, and Santa Anna's Pack-train Gold.* Little Rock: August House, 1991.

"Jefferson's Haunted Hotels and B&Bs." *All Info About Texas.* 22 Mar. 2006<http://texas.allinfoabout.com/cities/Jefferson_ghosts.html>.

Kahn, Kara. "Stories: Speed Walker." *Obiwan's UFO-Free Paranormal Pages.* 5 Apr. 2001. 13 Mar. 2006<http://www.ghosts.org/stories/tales/speed-walker.html>.

Kelso, John. *Texas Curiosities: Strangely Fascinating People, Places, and Things.* Guilford, Connecticut: Globe Pequot Press, 2000.

"Knottingley born Old West Gunfighter Ben Thompson." *Knottingley & Ferrybridge Online.* Knottingley.org. 13 Mar. 2006<http://www.knottingley.org/history/ben_ thompson.htm>.

Krauss, Beth. Personal interview. 27 Mar. 2006.

Metz, Leon C. *Roadside History of Texas.* Missoula, Montana: Mountain Press Publishing Company, 1994.

Moneyhon, Carl H. "Davis, Edmund Jackson." *Handbook of Texas Online.* 6 June 2001. Texas State Historical Association. 7 Mar. 2006<http://www.tsha.utexas.edu/ handbook/online/articles/DD/fda37.html>.

Nalewicki, Jennifer. "Ghost Town: Tour reveals the paranormal side of Austin's history." *Daily Texan Online* 31 Oct. 2001. 1 Mar. 2006<http://www.dailytexanonline. com/media/storage/paper410/news/2001/10/30/Focus/ Ghost.Town-504719.shtml?norewrite200609071121&so urcedomain=www.dailytexanonline.com>.

Owen, Charles Brian. "Seiders Springs." *Bryker Woods Neighborhood Association*. Texas Hill Country Information Service. 31 Mar. 2006<http://www.txinfo.com/brykerwoods/Parks/SeiderSprings.html>.

"Partial View of Austin, Texas / 1890-1895 c." Map. *Archives & Manuscripts*. 1895. Texas State Library and Archives Commission. 3 Aug. 2006<http://www.tsl.state.tx.us/cgi-bin/aris/maps/maplookup.php3?mapnum=0926e>.

"Paying Final Respects." *KXAN.com* 28 May 2004, Text - News 36 video ed. 29 Apr. 2006<http://www.kxan.com/global/story.asp?s=1904847&ClientType=Printable>.

Permenter, Paris. *Shifra Stein's day trips from San Antonio and Austin*. Old Saybrook, Connecticut: Globe Pequot Press, 1997.

"Plan of the City of Austin / 1853." Map. *Archives & Manuscripts*. 1853. Texas State Library and Archives Commission. 14 July 2006<http://www.tsl.state.tx.us/cgi-bin/aris/maps/maplookup.php3?mapnum=0928>.

Quigley, Ian. "The Fantastic and Utterly Disreputable History of the Bevy of Sin Known as Guy Town: Before

It Was the Warehouse District, It Was the Whorehouse District." *The Austin Chronicles* 26 Jan. 2001, Features ed. 21 Mar. 2006<http://www.austinchronicle.com/gyrobase/Issue/story?oid=oid%3A80321>.

"Revised Map of Austin, Texas / 1885." Map. *Archives & Manuscripts*. 1885. Texas State Library and Archives Commission. 25 July 2006<http://www.tsl.state.tx.us/cgi-bin/aris/maps/maplookup.php3?mapnum=2283>.

"SanJacinto-Museum.org." *The San Jacinto Museum of History*. The San Jacinto Museum of History. 14 Mar. 2006<http://http://www.sanjacinto-museum.org/>.

Saylor, Steven. *A Twist at the End: A Novel of O. Henry*. New York, New York: Simon & Schuster, 2000.

"The Servant Girl Annihilator - Austin, TX." *American Terror*. 8 July 2003. 8 Sept. 2006<http://www.americanterror.com/info.cfm?id=56&state=TX>.

"The Shoal Creek Greenbelt." Map. *RunTex, the Runner's Store*. 2005. Edward Tasch. 7 Sept. 2006<http://www.runtex.com/shoalcreek_2006.pdf>.

Smith, Cheryl. "In Memoriam: The Austin State Hospital Cemetery is the long final home for thousands." *The Austin Chronicle* 27 May 2005. 24 Mar. 2006<http://www.austinchronicle.com/gyrobase/Issue/story?oid=oid%3A272559>.

Song, Gil. "Austin Landmarks Claim Haunted History." *The Daily Texan* 31 Oct. 2003. 12 July 2006<http://media. www.dailytexanonline.com/media/storage/paper410/news/2003/10/31/StateLocal/Austin.Landmarks.Claim. Haunted.History-545085.shtml?>.

[Spaghetti Warehouse staff], David. Personal interview. 27 Mar. 2006.

"Speakeasy - Austin Texas - live music." *Speakeasy.* 2005. 1 Mar. 2006<http://speakeasyaustin.com/history.html>.

"Speakeasy History / Speakeasy Fact." Speakeasy - Austin Texas - live music. Speakeasy.com. 1 Mar. 2006<http://speakeasyaustin.com/history.html>.

"Stage Stop Ranch." *Stage Stop Ranch.* 14 Mar. 2006<http://www.stagestopranch.com>.

Stapleton, Clayton. "Austin's Lady in Blue." *What Was Then.* 9 Mar. 2003. 28 Feb. 2006<http://www.whatwasthen. com/ladyinblue.html>.

—. "The Driskill Hotel." *What Was Then*. 11 July 2005. 28
  Mar. 2006<http://www.whatwasthen.com/driskill.html>.

—. "The Gonzales Clock Tower - The Cursed Clock." *What
  Was Then*. 7 Nov. 2003. 4 Aug. 2006<http://http://www.
  whatwasthen.com/clock.html>.

—. "Haunted Capitol." *What Was Then*. 19 Jan. 2003. 28
  Feb. 2006<http://www.whatwasthen.com/haunted_
  capitol.htm>.

—. "The Moore's Crossing Bridge." *What Was Then*. 28
  Mar. 2003. 28 Feb. 2006<http://www.whatwasthen.com/
  moorescrossing.html>.

—. "The Servant Girl Annihilator." *What Was Then*. 11
  July 2005. 12 July 2006<http://www.whatwasthen.com/
  ripper.htm>.

—. "Texas Governor's Mansion." *What Was Then*. 13 Apr.
  2004. 28 Feb. 2006<http://www.whatwasthen.com/
  governors_mansion.htm>.

—. "201 East Pecan Street." *What Was Then*. 14 July 2004.
  28 Feb. 2006<http://www.whatwasthen.com/missouri.
  html>.

Stapleton, K. C. "The Tavern." *What Was Then*. 15 July 2003. 28 Feb. 2006<http://www.whatwasthen.com/the_ tavern1.htm>.

Stein, Bill. "Colorado County Feud." *Handbook of Texas Online*. Texas State Historical Association. 19 July 2006<http://www.tsha.utexas.edu/handbook/online/ articles/CC/jcc7_print.html>.

—. Historic tour of Columbus, Texas city cemetery. Texas Paranormal Researchers. Columbus, TX. 15 July 2006.

Stucco, Johnny. "Drive-by Architecture: The Paramount Theater (1915)." *Texas Escapes* Sept. 2001. 1 Mar. 2006<http://www.texasescapes.com/AustinTexas/ ParamountTheatre/AustinParamountTheatre.htm>.

"Texas Historic Hotels—The Driskill Hotel Historic Timeline." *The Driskill Hotel*. 2005. 9 May 2006<http:// www.driskillhotel.com/about_timeline.html>.

"Top Haunted Spots on Austin Citysearch." *Citysearch*. 3 Mar. 2006<http://austin.citysearch.com/ roundup/40468>.

Turner, Ken. Description of 'ghost paintings' and gallery history. Texas Paranormal Researchers. Turner-Chapman Gallery, Columbus, TX. 15 July 2006.

"University of Texas Old Main, Austin." *Emporis Buildings*. Emporis. 12 Sept. 2006<http://www.emporis.com/en/wm/bu/?id=169147>.

"Viewing Bats in Texas." *Welcome to Bat Conservation International*. 2006. Bat Conservation International. 27 Feb. 2006<http://www.batcon.org/home/index.asp?idPage=90>.

Walsh, Mary Jayne. "Driskill, Jesse Lincoln." *Handbook of Texas Online*. Texas State Historical Association. 1 Mar. 2006<http://tsha.utexas.edu/handbook/online/articles/DD/fdr6.html>.

Weaver, Casey. *Austin Postcard*. 2002. 10 June 2006<http://www.austinpostcard.com/index.html>.

Williams, Docia Schultz. *Best Tales of Texas Ghosts*. Plano,
    TX: Republic of Texas Press, 1998.

Willoughby, Larry. *Austin: A Historical Portrait*. Norfolk, VA:
    Donning, 1997.

Zelade, Richard. "A Columbus History." *Richard Zelade's
    Website*. 14 July 2006<http://www.io.com/~xeke/
    columbushistory.htm>.

—. "Contemplated Servile Rising in Texas." *Richard Zelade's
    Website*. The Galveston news. 7 Sept. 2006<http://www.
    io.com/~xeke/columbushistory.htm>.

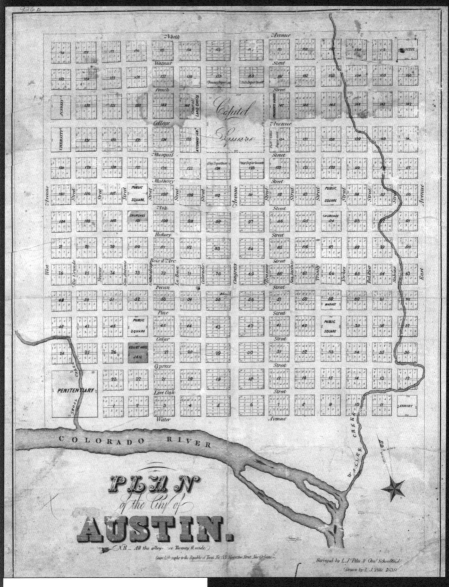

Plan for the City of Austin, ca. 1839.

Early twentieth century Austin postcard image.

THE CAPITOL AT AUSTIN.

Austin's Capitol Building, 1879, four years before Governor Davis began haunting it.

Congress Avenue, Austin, Texas

Early postcard of Congress Avenue.

Annie Oakley represented the hardy women of the Wild West.

INDEX

For additional information about ghost hunting, visit
Hollow Hill, http://www.HollowHill.com/

For updates about Austin's ghosts and related topics, see
The Ghosts of Austin, Texas website,
http://www.Ghosts-Austin.com/

To contact the author, write to

Fiona Broome
Fiona@HollowHill.com